BIODYNAMIC GARDENING

FOR HEALTH & TASTE

HILARY WRIGHT

Floris Books

To Graham and Geoff, the Legomen
And for Sophia, who was very insistent

First published in 2003 by Mitchell Beazley

This edition published in 2009 by Floris Books
Second printing 2013

British Library CIP Data available
ISBN: 978-086315-696-0
Printed in China

Contents

What is biodynamics? 6

Working with the rhythms of nature 26

Harnessing the power of the zodiac 40

Herbal tonics for your garden 52

Biodynamic composting 66

Natural pest and disease control 80

Putting it into practice 90

Biodynamics in the kitchen 112

Intuitive gardening 120

Biodynamics and the future 128

Resources directory 136

Index 142

Acknowledgments 144

What is biodynamics?

What a long way we've come. In recent decades organic gardening has shot from obscurity to front-page news. Not so long ago organic food was only available in health-food shops, often at great expense. Now it's for sale in every supermarket. The prices may still be high, but at least the food is available.

But . . . have you noticed how sometimes even organic vegetables and fruit still don't taste of anything? It's great that we can buy food without having to worry that it might have been sprayed with carcinogenic chemicals. It's marvellous that we can support farmers who are growing our food

responsibly, with minimum damage to the countryside. It's inescapable, though, that this food will be grown with commercial values in mind. A lettuce grown organically in a polytunnel will still lack the flavour of food grown in the open air, in its season. And commercial growers frequently choose varieties according to uniformity of size and ripening – to make produce easier to sell – rather than for maximum taste and flavour, which is the home gardener's imperative. After all, farmers still have to get the goods to market, and persuade hard-nosed supermarket buyers that their produce has "eye appeal."

Anyone who's ever grown their own vegetables knows how much better food tastes when it comes directly from the garden into the kitchen. At one time my garden consisted solely of a window box bursting with lettuces and herbs and a balcony full of tomato plants in growbags, and I prized that food above anything I could buy. I picked those tomatoes a few at a time, when they were perfectly ripe, and they were on the table being eaten within minutes of leaving the plant.

Given that we're now so conscious of the importance of organic agriculture, it seems amazing to think back to the first British television series on organic gardening, which was broadcast in 1987. It was called *All Muck and Magic*, maybe because it was thought the public would find the idea of making compost, and growing food without chemicals, too weird and wacky. Now we take it for granted that this is the healthy way to produce our food.

That means that the time may be ripe to look even further back, past the origins of organic gardening, to an even earlier model, one that really does have the whiff of magic about it. "Magic" because not only are the results truly magical, but because there's a good measure of what seems like hocus-pocus attached to the practice of biodynamic gardening.

LEFT *Superb biodynamic tomatoes can be grown anywhere – this attractive terracotta pot saves space on a patio or balcony. Parsley is a good companion for tomatoes – add it to the pot for extra bug protection.*

Restoring fertility

Stories about the decline in human fertility hit today's newspapers and magazines with depressing regularity. Some of us have already experienced these difficulties on a personal level. Many blame the increased use of hormone-based chemicals in animal rearing and organophosphate chemicals sprayed on agricultural land. Sooner or later these chemicals end up in the human body, and scientists are already pointing to a causal connection – cause and effect – between these chemicals and human inability to conceive, birth defects, and maybe even modern diseases such as attention deficit disorder and fibromyalgia.

These problems have cast a shadow over the earth for over a hundred years. As long ago as 1924 a group of concerned farmers got together in Germany to address the problem of the decline in soil and animal fertility they were experiencing, a decline brought about, they believed, by intensive farming. They turned to Rudolf Steiner (1861–1925), an Austrian scientist and clairvoyant, who gave a series of lectures laying down new ground rules for rescuing soil fertility and with it, in the long run, maybe human life itself.

Steiner believed that people had done so much damage to the earth, through over-intensive farming and use of chemical poisons, that it was nothing like enough to build a compost heap and stop spraying chemicals, valuable though these actions were. He took a wider view. He gave new meaning to the term "holistic," because his view of the whole extended past the soil and beyond the sun to the moon and the planets – the entire cosmos. He saw it all as a unified interconnected process and started the ball rolling with ways to work with all these energies.

Steiner also focused on the use of plants as healing agents – notably with plants that often grow like weeds, such as nettles and camomile. He recommended various ways of using these plants to rebuild soil fertility and even gave a method for using cow manure in a way no-one had previously imagined (*see pp.53–65*).

Simple, but not easy

This is where the accusation of "hocus-pocus" creeps in. And it's also where things get very complicated indeed. Steiner laid down a series of "indications" or suggestions on what might be done, but didn't give clear step-by-step instructions to follow. After he died, his believers carried out extensive research and experimentation, and sometimes their conclusions collided. From these

collisions sprang orthodoxies, and some people started to codify how things should be done, based on their results. There are apparently several ways to skin a cat, though why anyone would try I can't imagine, and there are many nuances to applying the principles of biodynamics.

What has been lacking until now is a simple way of getting started. When I first became interested in biodynamics I had a difficult time trying to grapple with these rather esoteric concepts and work out exactly what to do and when to do it. Biodynamics invites you to work the land in a very different way to chemical-based or even organic methods: to observe the garden more closely, work with nature's rhythms, plant according to the zodiac, and spray some rather unusual herbal remedies on the plants and garden.

It took me a while to get used to all these new concepts. Some of the ideas seemed pretty mind-boggling. But as I began to actually work with them, rather than just read about them, they started to make sense. And I noticed some profound changes in my self and in my attitude towards the garden. I became increasingly aware of what was going on in the garden and felt far more attuned to my little patch of land. I began to realize what was needed in order for the plants to really thrive.

Surprise, surprise, the garden flourished as never before. And as it flourished, so my pleasure in gardening grew. I noticed a power in the plants that simply hadn't been there before, an amazing vibrancy and vitality. It was just as unsurprising that this sense of vitality accompanied the harvested fruit and

LEFT *Whatever you decide to grow, biodynamic techniques, such as choosing the right time to plant and nourishing the soil with herbal remedies, will help you achieve excellent results.*

vegetables into the kitchen and onto the plate. They smelled better. They tasted better. And I am convinced that they did me a lot more good than bought produce.

This book builds on and extends organic gardening methods, and if you already follow organic principles, you're well on the way to enjoying biodynamic gardening. Another example of this extension principle is in medicine: Steiner developed various healing practices that can be added onto a training in modern Western medicine, each aspect informing and enhancing the other.

I am no expert, but I feel passionately that biodynamics has made a difference in my garden. I've explained the key underlying principles and given practical, easy-to-follow ways to begin gardening biodynamically. I do believe, however, that a grasp of the basic theory will aid understanding of the practical instructions, so the two will go hand in hand.

There's no place like your garden

In biodynamics it is believed that there is nowhere else on the planet like your garden, with its own precise combination of soil, microclimate, and microorganisms – what the French call *terroir*, a unique sense of place. The simple act of cultivating changes the landscape. As you interact with your garden, no matter how small, you put your stamp on it and contribute to its individuality. Nobody else will be able to produce fruit and vegetables that taste quite like yours, and this uniqueness will spur your enthusiasm. What could be better than eating food grown in your unique garden?

Learning from past mistakes

That picture of unique sense of place was one that I treasured as being part of agriculture in times gone by, so it was a shock to discover that there has never really been a "golden age" of agriculture, where man and nature worked in harmony to produce the food we needed while protecting the planet. Not in the West, at least. Although the Chinese had for thousands of years maintained soil fertility through careful composting of animal and vegetable wastes, when John Constable (1776–1837) painted his iconic image of bucolic Englishness, *The Haywain*, in 1821, Europe was already well on the way to destroying that image.

Agriculture began in prehistoric times, about nine or ten thousand years ago, when man gave up the hunter-gatherer nomadic way of life. This transition is even reflected in The Bible – Cain, the first farmer, slew his brother Abel, who was a nomadic shepherd – a violent metaphor for the new way supplanting the old. Neolithic farmers arrived in Britain from the Mediterranean *c.*3500 BC and felled woodland to make room for fields of crops

and animals. It took them just a few hundred years to degrade the land so completely that it would barely support sheep, and the denuded soils simply blew away. Soil erosion, the problem that removes millions of tons of topsoil from once-fertile land every year, is sadly nothing new.

Animal manure, the bedrock of soil fertility, was in short supply – most animals were slaughtered at the end of the grass-growing season each year, because there wasn't enough fodder to overwinter livestock. Soil fertility slid ever further into decline, at least until medieval times when a series of disastrous famines paved the way for the Black Death of the 14th century, a plague that killed up to half of Britain's population. With the subsequent shortage of peasants to work the fields, once-arable land returned to grazing, and sheep farming became popular, largely because it demanded less labour. Wool became a highly profitable export commodity, so much so that big landowners, such as greedy feudal lords and the Catholic Church, forced thousands of people off their common lands to make way for vast sheepwalks.

BELOW *This weathered brick wall is more than decorative – it provides a windbreak, protecting tender plants from wind chill and damage, giving earlier, larger crops.*

After a few hundred years under grass, aided by animal manure, soil fertility improved again. The Industrial Revolution brought about huge migrations of population from country to city, with dispossessed peasants-turned-slum-dwellers needing food. The first stirrings of the new "scientific age" in the 18th century brought results in agriculture. The English agriculturist Jethro Tull (1674–1741) invented the seed drill, and at the same time a four-year crop rotation was created, new seed varieties were developed, and livestock were bred for increased productivity. The importance of humus (the organic constituent of soil) came to be understood, as did the use of legumes for green manure.

These discoveries were soon put into profitable practice. Market gardeners, newly based on the edges of cities, engaged in the very lucrative trade of carting in food to new city markets. Many of these market gardeners utilized the French intensive bed system invented in Paris, where growers had put the huge amounts of horse manure generated by the city's transport system to work as the basis for growing more food in a small but well-fertilized space.

The population explosion in the cities led to fears that demand for food would outstrip supply. To counteract this, cheap meat and grain supplies were imported from the colonies – an action that worked against British growers; undercut by these cheaper colonial supplies many farmers went bankrupt, and nearly 800,000ha (two million acres) of arable land yet again reverted to grassland.

Even this enforced soil replenishment didn't help, as soil fertility was in decline again. But this time, the new scientific age seemed to have the answer. Justus von Liebig (1803–73), known as the "father of agricultural chemistry,"

ABOVE *Container-grown plants benefit from first-class compost. Use the special biodynamic composting techniques to produce nourishing compost that will support plants growing in restricted spaces.*

discovered the need to replace elements taken from the soil when harvesting crops. He saw no need to distinguish between nitrogen in organic form from manure and nitrogen in the form of chemical salts. While it was a good thing to discover and analyze the chemical constituents of soil, the drawback was that scientists came to think that only chemicals mattered, that crops were nothing more than commodities requiring chemical inputs and providing nutritional outputs.

This materialistic world-view stemmed from the philosopher René Descartes (1596–1650), who promoted faith in analytical reasoning, seeing the world as a machine. His thinking influenced Isaac Newton (1642–1727), who developed a mechanistic view of the world, seen strictly in terms of cause and effect. He famously discovered gravity when an apple fell on his head, but he didn't

LEFT *For centuries, life was intimately connected with the land. Work followed the seasons, and people understood the rhythms of nature. Is it not time to reclaim what has been lost since moving away from the land?*

consider the possibility of gravity's opposite polarity, levity. In other words, gravity is what made the apple fall on his head; levity is what put the apple up there in the first place and it is what enables plants to defy gravity and grow upwards. Science operates in terms of polar opposites – light and dark, hot and cold, positive and negative – but it ignores the opposite pole to gravity.

This mechanistic, materialist philosophy found an opposing voice in the poets of the Romantic movement. The foremost representative of this world-view was the poet and dramatist Johann Wolfgang von Goethe (1749–1832), whose last years were devoted to a now-forgotten study of science. Goethe developed a theory of colour that refuted Newton's, and he also became a dedicated botanist. He emphasized the need for meticulous observation, during which one should not attempt to separate oneself from nature – a view that ran entirely contrary to the prevailing scientific standpoint. He was probably the first scientist to take a "holistic" approach to the natural world.

The alchemists also opposed a materialist view. They had searched since Egyptian times for the Philosopher's Stone, the means by which they could transmute any base metal into gold. Despite the charlatans who jumped on the bandwagon and duped gullible peasants with promises of gold, many alchemists were spiritual seekers, aware of the oneness of creation and searching for spiritual transformation; they were persecuted by the church for their beliefs.

Scientists had distanced themselves from the holistic approach by the 19th century, and the discoveries of the materialist sciences had a profound effect on the world. During World War I German scientists discovered how to "fix" nitrogen from the air to make explosives. After the war the same technology was diverted to producing nitrogen for fertilizers. Tanks, another invention from World War I, became the basis of technology for tractor-building. The poison gases employed to such deadly effect in the trenches were used as the basis for the first pesticides.

World War II also brought with it many technological developments for agriculture from warfare, some of which continue to damage the planet to this day. The noxious insecticide DDT, for instance, won its creator, the Swiss chemist Paul Müller, the Nobel prize in 1944, and the Germans developed organophosphates as part of their chemical weapons research. Britain was finally forced to stop importing food during the war, when Atlantic shipping lines were cut off by German U-boats; the population was urged to "Dig for Victory," and Britain rediscovered the vegetable plot.

After the war, devastated European economies were aided by Americans via the Marshall Plan, which fostered increased mechanization. Agriculture came to be viewed as just another industrial process and one a good deal less lucrative than factory jobs in cities – magnets that pulled farm labourers off the land in droves. The farmer became ever more isolated from other farm workers, and from the land itself. (Patrolling the land 1m (3ft) off the ground while sitting in a Land Rover or tractor isn't the same as walking the earth.) The best fertilizer is said to be a farmer's footprints – that's a view that is completely at odds with the intensive fertilizer and pesticide programmes most modern farmers use today.

Modern machinery demands straight-edged fields, so that the land can be worked in efficient straight lines; today the countryside is made up of huge fields, with stretches of hedgerows grubbed up, bird and animal habitats removed, and farmland exposed to increased risk of soil erosion.

Rudolf Steiner

Even after only a few years of these chemical inputs it became apparent that damage was being done. A group of farmers in 1920s eastern Germany observed that the introduction of chemical fertilizers had already, in just one generation, led to depleted soils and a decline in the fertility and health of both animals and crops. It happened that these farmers were anthroposophists, adherents of the movement founded by Steiner.

LEFT *Isaac Newton realized that it was gravity that caused the apple to fall. Biodynamics looks at what causes the apple to be up there in the first place.*

Steiner was born in rural Austria in 1861, a time when the old world of peasant wisdom and working with the rhythms of nature was colliding with the new world of science and technical understanding. His genius lay in his ability to synthesize these two warring worlds, studying first philosophy and science then integrating this knowledge with his innate clairvoyant spirituality and the folk wisdom he learned in childhood. Out of this evolved anthroposophy (*anthropo* = human being, *sophia* = wisdom), meaning the inherent wisdom of humanity. His mindset and philosophy is remarkably relevant today, because he wanted people neither to veer off towards rampant materialism and consumerism, nor to float around on new age clouds, disconnected from the world. His idea of balance was to move past superstition on the one hand and dogmatic belief in science on the other, to observe rationally, and also allow everything to be permeated with the spirit.

Steiner wrote copiously on a number of esoteric subjects, and his work has many practical applications today, including a very successful system of education known as the Waldorf or Steiner schools, medicine, eurythmy (a system of movements that makes speech visible), and the Camphill communities, which care for adults with learning difficulties (*see pp.136–7*). He was also the catalyst for a re-evaluation of Goethe's scientific work, devoting many years of his life to editing Goethe's scientific writings.

LEFT Alchemists sought to transmute the base into the pure, turning base metals into gold, and also to purify and improve the self. Gardeners turn rotting fruit and grass cuttings into nourishing compost – another form of alchemy.

The beginning of biodynamics

A group of German anthroposophist-farmers begged Steiner to help them develop a programme for healing the land, and eventually he delivered a series of lectures to around 60 of these farmers in Koberwitz, Silesia, in 1924.

The eight lectures were transcribed and published under the title *Spiritual Foundations for the Renewal of Agriculture*, known familiarly as *Agriculture* or "The Ag. Course" or "The Ag. Lectures." The book is not an easy read and coming to it without any preparation was nearly enough to put me off biodynamics for ever. Almost, but not quite. Steiner was speaking to a group of farming experts already intimately acquainted with his anthroposophical ideas, so he took a great deal of knowledge for granted and spoke to them at an appropriately high level.

Many students of biodynamics spend a lifetime studying this book, and experimenting with different ways of putting the sometimes infuriatingly vague "indications" Steiner gave into practice. He died not long after delivering the lectures, so in many cases there was incomplete information – very often he gave his followers the outline of an idea and told them they must experiment to find out what worked in practice.

Biodynamics has been full of experimenters ever since. Steiner's work was almost eradicated when the Nazis came to power in 1933, but, fortunately, several key adherents emigrated to Britain (Eugen and Lilly Kolisko) or to the USA (Ehrenfried Pfeiffer). Worldwide experimentation continued apace after World War II ended.

Biodynamics today

Surely what the world needs now is a swift, simple, effective means of healing the land. The odd thing is that while there are thriving biodynamic farms all over the Western world, biodynamics isn't well known. One of the reasons for this may be that, as with many bodies of knowledge received from a wise man or woman, diverging orthodoxies develop from those original words.

This means that some of the literature on biodynamics is complicated and, at times, contradictory. Several introductory books, on the other hand, leave out so much of the story that the reader can't help but conclude that there isn't much difference between biodynamics and organics. The aim of this book is to distil the essential principles and present them in as straightforward a way as possible. Why? Because, as Steiner himself said in *Agriculture*, "The most important

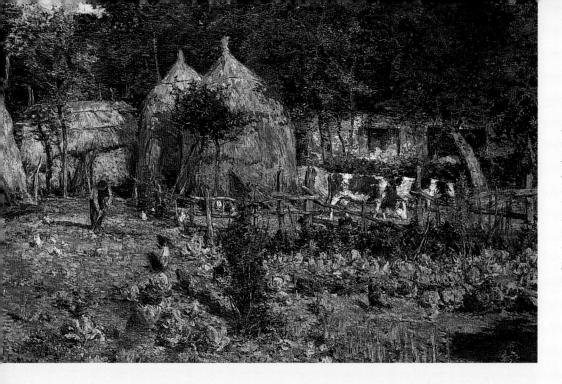

thing is to make the benefits of our agricultural preparations available to the largest possible areas over the entire Earth, so that the Earth may be healed and the nutritive quality of its produce improved in every respect." He wanted the information he had given to the farmers to be disseminated far and wide.

There are other possible reasons for biodynamics' relative obscurity. In the materialist decades that followed World War II, with the emphasis largely on technology, the space race, and widespread industrialization of agriculture, biodynamics might have seemed akin to witchcraft. We may not believe in the superstitions of medieval times, but many people still reject out of hand what can't be proved by the five senses. Biodynamists may simply have preferred to keep their heads down, avoid publicity, and just get on with healing.

Nor are there many economic opportunities in selling to those who practise biodynamics. Organic growers do present sales opportunities – witness the stacks of sacks of organic potting compost and "organic" bug sprays on sale in garden centres – but all biodynamics needs in terms of input are tiny amounts of a few herbal preparations. Scientific research funding for universities and agricultural colleges is often closely linked to commercial companies, so it's not surprising that biodynamics is not mentioned much in academia.

Despite being a fairly well-kept secret, however, biodynamics is discreetly practised all over the world, which means that people must be finding that the results are worth the effort. Not surprisingly, it is strong in Europe, especially Germany and Britain, but it also has many adherents in Australia, New Zealand,

and the USA. Pioneering work is being done with biodynamics in India, with extremely successful results in adapting the principles to the tropics. And some of France's top winemakers now use biodynamics to make even finer wine.

How is biodynamics different from organics?

Biodynamic gardening has a lot in common with organic gardening practices. Both reject the use of toxic chemicals on the land and believe first and foremost in building a healthy soil, seeing it as the key to fertility.

Conventional organic practices encompass the use of green manures, cover crops, regular cultivation, composting, and companion planting. Biodynamics embraces all of these as sensible aspects of ecologically sound gardening, but it recognizes that soil and animal fertility continue to decline, and there is a need to do more than simply feed the soil – the earth itself needs to be healed. Biodynamics therefore goes a step or two beyond organics, seeking to heal the earth through the use of a series of remedies applied to the soil, to the leaves of plants, and to the compost pile. This is the main thing separating biodynamics from organics – plus the spiritual element, the "dynamic" side of the equation.

LEFT *Organic produce is flown in from all over the world to grace supermarket shelves. However, does food that has come from so far afield, and eaten out of season, actually taste of anything?*

This dynamic side involves metaphysical ideas such as increasing vital life-force, known as "chi" to the Chinese (as in chi kung or t'ai chi), "prana" to the Indians, and "mana" to the Hawaiians. Forms of Chinese energy medicine such as acupuncture involve removing the blocks to the natural flow of energy or life-force through the body. The Chinese use a complex system of meridians, energy lines that they have identified as running throughout the body and connecting with major organs. Western medicine has been unable to find a scientifically acceptable explanation of why acupuncture works, and yet it continues to be effective.

Plants need a great many trace elements, which cannot easily be supplied by chemical fertilizers as they prove toxic in large amounts. Organic methods offer plants these elements in the right amounts. Steiner went further, believing that these elements are borne on wind and rain, available to any plant at any time if it has sufficient life-force to be able to capture and absorb them.

Steiner insisted that his system for improving the life-force in plants was not an article of faith, something to be taken on trust and blindly believed. He encouraged scientific experimentation to test the effectiveness of what he suggested, and trials of certain aspects of his work have been ongoing for decades. I think, however, that a pragmatic approach will bring results. Experts may not agree, but I don't think that you have to believe in the underlying theory to make effective use of the ideas in practice and get outstanding results in your garden.

In a powerful version of "think globally, act locally," biodynamics encourages gardeners to become aware of everything that can influence plant growth, from deep inside the earth to the far reaches of the cosmos. It takes a view diametrically opposed to conventional, chemical-based agriculture, which sees both plants and soil as inert items needing chemical inputs in order to maximize their output as nutritional vehicles. Biodynamics believes that the soil itself should be alive and that

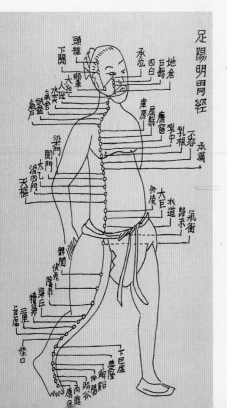

LEFT *Chinese medicine recognizes 14 major meridians, or energy lines, flowing through the body, connecting major organs. The free flow of energy along the meridians maintains health.*

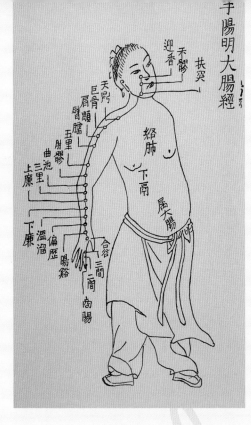

the degree to which the soil is alive will affect the vibrancy and health of the plants it supports. Gardeners are asked to undertake detailed, patient, careful, long-term observations of nature, and invited to become keenly aware of the effects of sun, rainfall, warmth, and cold on their unique patch of land. They observe in minute detail what happens when the land is sprayed with special biodynamic remedies. Biodynamics even involves them using their intuition, to "tune in" to the garden and become aware of what's happening at an entirely new and deep level.

LEFT *Asian practices such as acupuncture and shiatsu work on key points along the meridians to keep energy, "chi", flowing freely along them.* OPPOSITE PAGE *stomach meridian;* LEFT *large intestine meridian.*

Steiner's ideal – the farm

Biodynamics is ideally practised as a completely self-supporting farm unit, like an organism. Animals would be fed by the farm, and their manure used to form the basis of the compost process, to which would be added weeds, kitchen scraps, dead flowers, and dropped leaves, all of which would magically be recycled in the composting process and given back to the earth in the form of life-giving humus. Thus it becomes a unique, individual entity. Such a farm ideally produces more than it needs and so can give back to the local community.

Naturally this ideal is not practical for most of us, who want to garden on a scale to feed ourselves but not necessarily devote every waking hour to doing so (and just think of the size of back garden you'd need to graze a cow…). Gardeners can work with the underlying concept of the self-sufficient farm, though, by following the principles of recycling with whatever materials come to hand.

Proof of the pudding

Prove it, you say. Well, many studies have been carried out, such as the 21-year study in Switzerland that quantified some of the benefits of biodynamics. Some people believe the results they've gained in their own gardens and are not interested in proof printed in a scientific journal; others won't believe anything without such proof. We all have our own ways of deciding what is true, but there

is one important point to bear in mind: science can't measure everything yet. We can't see radio waves but that doesn't mean they don't exist. A modern view of science is that it's all part of the same whole, that everything on the planet – you, me, that spade, this tomato – is created out of the same basic building block: energy. Once you have grasped that, the theory goes, you'll understand everything. It's all interwoven, and everything depends on everything else.

Nor is science what it used to be. What I learnt at school a generation ago has been reviewed, updated, and amended. There's a different set of "facts" nowadays. Science isn't a smooth procession of logically evolving discoveries, each securely built on the one that went before. It's more like lurching from one point of view to another, wildly differing point of view, with each new orthodoxy coming to obliterate the old. Think of Galileo endorsing Copernicus's theory that the earth revolves around the sun. In Galileo's time it was heresy to believe such a thing.

ABOVE *Some of the world's finest vineyards use biodynamic gardening methods to produce top-quality grapes. This vineyard in the Vaucluse, France, has interplanted the vines with phacelia, which attracts beneficial insects such as bees, hoverflies, and lacewings. Its roots help break up hard soil.*

Nowadays even creationists accept that the sun is the centre of our universe; but five hundred years ago the entire Catholic Church's cosmogony was built on the belief that the earth is the centre of the universe, and it did not suit the pope to change this view. Centuries on we shouldn't be smug about this attitude to knowledge. Our current orthodoxies are every bit as susceptible to being swept away in the light of new knowledge that could be just around the corner. Maybe the knowledge, the wisdom, and awareness that biodynamics is built on will come to be an everyday truth. The question that has most validity, I think, is not "is it true?" but "does it work?" And that's a question each of us can answer for ourselves in the privacy of our own vegetable patch.

The science of the biodynamic garden

Nowhere is this different approach more evident than in the biodynamic approach to the chemical constituents of the garden.

Carbon

Humans, animals, plants, and minerals are carbon-based life forms. Carbon forms our basic framework, giving us rigidity – the hardest known substance, diamond, is pure carbon.

Oxygen

Oxygen is our life-force; it's in all living things, taken from the air we breathe. Water that does not contain dissolved oxygen is unable to support life.

Nitrogen

Steiner saw nitrogen as forming a bridge between the life-force of oxygen and the rigidity and inertness of carbon. A group of plants, the legumes (plants that produce pods, such as peas and beans), are used to "fix" nitrogen, i.e. their roots capture nitrogen from the air and bring it down into the soil where it is deposited for subsequent crops to utilize. It is often clear to see when a garden has been fed chemical fertilizers: the growth is lush and watery, and there is too much leaf and stem growth and not enough flower or root growth. Aphids and fungus love lush, watery growth, so the plants are ripe for attack.

Hydrogen

The lightest of the elements. Steiner called hydrogen the "dissolver," dissolving forms.

Calcium

Calcium is connected, in biodynamics, with the forces of the earth, supporting soil structure. It is held to work with the forces of the moon.

Silica

Silica is the constituent element of sand (and glass). Because it is considered insoluble, it is disregarded in conventional garden chemistry – how, after all, could a plant absorb it? Yet all plants contain silica, so it must be taken into the plant somehow. Silica enables plants to stand up straight, toughening them against aphid and fungal attack.

Phosphorous

Important to help plants come to maturity in their growth cycle, i.e. to flower, fruit, and seed.

Potassium (potash)

Aids root development.

Working with the rhythms of nature

Has there ever been a time when we in the West have been so out of touch with the natural world? We live in towns or cities flooded by street lighting, blinded to the stars in the night sky, unable to tell a waxing from a waning moon, let alone recognize the constellations. Who wakes with the dawn chorus of birdsong these days, rather than an alarm clock? Most city dwellers can't even hear a dawn chorus any more. As we leap into the car to begin the school run or the commute to work we hardly even notice the weather, and some people drive from their garage to their place of work without stepping outside.

Most people don't grow their own fruit or vegetables, relying instead on food produced many hundreds or even thousands of miles away. Apples are picked green and "ripened" in glasshouses, for instance, and often they are irradiated to improve shelf life. The seeds of an irradiated apple can never germinate. It's a zombie apple, part of the living dead. What kind of lifeforce energy does eating an apple like this give us?

Eating food produced in a different part of the country, or even a different part of the world, gradually puts us out of touch with the cycle of the seasons. We've become so accustomed to finding anything we care to eat available to us at the supermarket, courtesy of air freighting and refrigeration, that we've lost the concept of "in season" completely. A generation or two ago, asparagus and strawberries were harbingers of summer and actually tasted of something. When was the last time you ate a strawberry that really tasted like a strawberry should?

When you garden for yourself you are immediately reminded that everything has a season. Biodynamics, with its intense study of the changing face of nature, allows nature's rhythms to move into sharper focus. We can learn to work with them, and to benefit from them, in unexpected ways.

Expansion and contraction

Biodynamics seeks to harness all available forces in order to heal and revitalize each individual patch of land. These forces include all of nature's rhythms, which form a constantly interacting, interdependent whole. The key to

BELOW *Walter Crane's painting shows the season moving in an ever-changing rhythm, the annual dance of birth, maturity, fruiting and death, cycling on round to rebirth.*

biodynamics is in its name: life-force energy, the fusion of the biological world and its dynamism, its endless change. Nothing in nature, nothing in life, remains static. Plants move through a cycle of leafing, flowering, fruiting, and dying. Animals and humans grow up, mature, reproduce, and finally die. It's a dynamic, constantly changing process.

Everything around us has dynamic cycles, too. There's a rhythm to the day-and-night cycle, to the seasonal growth unfolding throughout the year. It's a continuous cycle of expansion and contraction, which means that the earth itself can be seen as a single living organism. This may not be so easy for us to sense, trapped as we are on our own patch of earth with little ability to stand back and gain a larger perspective. But the astronauts on the moon experienced this feeling strongly when they viewed the earth from a distance of thousands of miles. Photographs of the earth taken from space are among the defining images of the 20th century. This sense of perspective, of seeing everything that is done in the garden as part of a larger whole, is one of the keys to working with biodynamics.

If you think of the earth as a single living entity, then imagine its circulation system being the water that's everywhere on the planet, endlessly transforming from rain to rivers to oceans to mists. The rhythm of the seasons acts like a pulse, expanding in spring and summer then contracting in autumn and winter. The skin, of course, consists of soil and plants. It's remarkable how nature repopulates barren soil with plant life. A newly weeded carrot patch quickly becomes clouded with weed seedlings, and in no time plants will push their way up through cracks in Tarmac, slag heaps, or even lava.

The earth's daily rhythm is the one that we live by; it expands in the morning with sunrise and contracting in the evening with sunset. What we call the "expansion rhythm" runs from 3am to 3pm, and the "contracting rhythm" from 3pm to 3am. For convenience, think of it as breathing out with the morning and relaxing in the afternoon with the in-breath. Flowers have their own daily rhythms, following the sun. Some flowers have rhythms so precise that you could almost set your watch by them, and indeed in earlier centuries flower clocks were planted for people to tell the time (*see p.33*).

These circadian rhythms affect us, too, more profoundly than modern life often allows us to acknowledge. Stepping out of sync, such as when crossing several time zones leads to jet lag, forces us to notice that we are, indeed, programmed to a particular daily rhythm.

Using daily rhythms in the garden

The idea that the earth has an out-breath each morning and an in-breath each evening can be harnessed for everyday gardening activity. Sap rises in the morning, so pick leafy vegetables and salads first thing, while they're at their

LEFT *The garden at dawn: my favourite time of day to be out and about, walking the land, observing the changes since yesterday, and harvesting the day's salads before the heat of the sun wilts them.*

freshest and most vital; later in the day they may well go limp. By contrast, take advantage of the sap falling again in the evening to pick root vegetables. By late afternoon onions, parsnips, or carrots will have received the full measure of the plant's life-force flowing back down to the roots as the earth contracts.

Annual rhythms – the sun

The sun is the giver of all life on earth, providing all the warmth and light we need to grow. Even though the earth moves around the sun, from our perspective – and a plant's – the sun moves around the centre of our personal universe, the earth. This is called a geocentric perspective.

As the sun moves through its annual cycle, as we perceive it, it rises higher in the sky from midwinter to midsummer. As it rises it draws plants up from the

earth, the expansive principle of levity in action. Then, after midsummer, the sun begins to wane and seems to drop gradually lower in the sky. Gravity reasserts itself as the earth contracts, receiving and drawing into itself the life-force the sun has given it during spring and summer. Gardeners now move into the harvest phase, gathering in the fruits of their labour and preparing for winter.

So the rhythms of the passing seasons are defined by the sun's annual transit. We say the sun rises in the east, but in fact it rises somewhere slightly different every day; a point south of east in the winter, moving to a point north of east in the summer. As it moves north, the days gradually lengthen, coming to a point where there is an equal (*equi*) length of day and night (*nox*): the equinox. At midsummer in the northern hemisphere, on the summer solstice, around June 21, the sun appears to stop moving for a moment before it begins its autumnal and winter journey back south. This is the solstice (*sol stetit*, Latin for "sun stands still").

It's significant that equinoxes and solstices, known as the cardinal points of the year, have been celebrated in the myth and ritual of many different cultures worldwide since ancient times. The equinoxes were observed as the borders between winter and summer, for instance. Every year Easter Sunday is set to fall on the first new moon after the spring equinox, a time when the levity principle is in full swing; plants are defying gravity and rising out of the earth, which is mirrored for Christians by the Resurrection.

The summer solstice, or the feast of St John, is the Midsummer Night that Shakespeare dreamed about, a night when it was believed that young girls could have visions of their future lover. In southern France I have witnessed villagers celebrating a St John's ritual that involved the young men walking through the flames of a bonfire. The winter solstice, when the sun again seems to stand still, was the moment when the ancients thought that the sun would never move again, and rituals were performed to propitiate the Sun God. Stonehenge, a megalithic monument in southwest England dating from 2000 BC, is just one of many stone circles aligned to receive the sun of the winter solstice. Native American peoples celebrated the solstice in sacred ritual. In ancient Egyptian temples the sun's solstice rays are focused into the inner sanctuaries. Ancient China, Japan, and Taiwan also had solstice ceremonies.

It is hardly surprising that when leaders of the Christian church came to fix a date for Jesus's birth they chose the first day after the solstice when the sun appeared to start moving again, carrying the potent symbolism that Jesus, the "Light of the World," was bringing the sun back to the earth. Indeed, in ancient calendars the solstice was reckoned as falling on 25 December and was celebrated as "the Nativity of the Sun".

LEFT *The sunflower's botanic name,* Helianthus, *celebrates its heliocentricity – the way it turns its head to the sun and follows the transit of the garden every day.*

Flower clock

Flower clocks originated in Sweden, devised by the famous naturalist Carl Linnaeus (1707–78), a professor at the university of Uppsala. In 1748, noticing the difference in the opening and closing times of various flowers, he planted his first clock or, as he called it, *horologium florae*. The clock was said to work well, even on cloudy days.

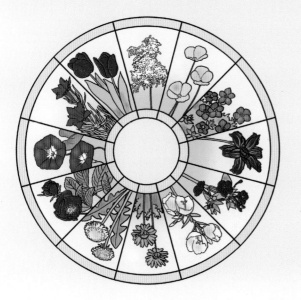

Some flower clock components:
(NB opening and closing times are approximate, depending on location)

Morning glory opens 5–6am

Sow thistle opens 6–7am

Dandelion opens 7–8am

African daisy opens 8–9am

Gentian opens 9–10am

Californian poppy opens 10–11am

Star of Bethlehem opens 11am

Morning glory closes noon

Star of Bethlehem closes 3pm

Californian poppy closes 4–5pm

Evening primrose opens 6pm

Dandelion closes 8–9pm

Nicotiana opens 9–10pm

Purple convolvulus opens 10–11pm

Night-flowering jasmine opens midnight

Winter

Most gardeners believe that this is the quietest time of the gardening year, when the earth lies dormant, and there's nothing to do but prune roses and read the seed catalogues. Biodynamics sees it differently. When the sun's shallow-angled rays pierce deep into the ground they enliven the soil, making it hum with life. The idea is that the life-forces from the sun are concentrated in the earth during winter, corresponding to the low angle of the sun's rays, which penetrate deep into the earth. Many animals feel this too, burrowing into the ground to hibernate. Frost and ice, the forces of crystallization, frequently penetrate the earth at this time, as well.

The first time I ever experienced a biodynamic garden – or rather, a vineyard – was in midwinter. A biting cold wind blew, and all around me stood dormant vines. Not a bud or a leaf in sight, yet the earth positively thrummed with life. That moment, everything I thought I knew about gardening turned on its head, and I was hooked. I had to know more.

LEFT *In spring the garden bursts with new life, as the forces of levity swing into action, encouraging upward growth. Waiting until the danger of frost is past before planting out tender vegetables saves much worry and time-consuming protective measures.*

LEFT *The upward growth of plants peaks at midsummer. Work in the garden takes up as much time as the gardener can offer, involving successional sowing, weeding, and harvesting. Take time to observe your garden, to sit and enjoy it and really notice all that's happening around you.*

Monthly rhythm – the moon

It is common knowledge that the moon controls tides as well as menstrual cycles, and that tides are higher at full moon, but the moon's influence is much further reaching than is immediately obvious. More babies are born at full moon than at new moon, and the same applies to many animals. Bees also have activity cycles linked to moon phase. The moon's influence works through the element of water. Wood cut close to full moon rots, because at this time the sap has risen to its highest, which makes it wetter. Timber is best cut close to the new moon, when sap has descended, making the wood less prone to rot. Herbs gathered at some times will have more curative power than those picked at other times.

This is definitely not "moonshine": the moon's effect on behaviour is undeniable. Even Charles Darwin (1809–82) acknowledged the influence of the moon on man, as well as on animals and plants. "Lunatic" originally meant someone who became mad intermittently, according to the phases of the moon. Police lay on extra staff at full moon, mental health units see more unrest in their patients, and, of course, we all know about werewolves. A waiter once remarked to me that his customers seemed to "go weird" at full moon, and that he could tell that the full moon was up by observing the changes in customers' behaviour. He wanted to leave his job every full moon. For many of us, the days approaching full moon bring increased sleeplessness or very vivid dreams.

Once upon a time folk wisdom was treasured and passed down from one generation to the next, keeping the people in touch with the rhythms of nature. It was only at the end of the 19th century, when chemistry was taking over agriculture and fostering a purely materialistic view of the farming process, that mechanization crept into other areas of life. For centuries it had been enough to tell the approximate time by the sun or even a flower clock. The coming of the railways changed all that. Local times, hundreds of them, were standardized into national time; Greenwich Mean Time was established in 1847. International time zones were drawn up and it became important to carry a watch.

The more machines and instruments people began to use, the less they valued the old ways of doing things, dismissing them as old-fashioned or, worse, superstition. The railways were just one manifestation of a speeded-up life, a life that continues to accelerate today. Learning about the moon's many rhythms offers a welcome shift of gears to a slower pace.

Moondance: many rhythms of the moon

The moon has several distinct cycles, all taking a little more or less than 27 days. The system is complicated but worth examining, because all of these cycles can turn up in the gardening year, as times when it's not a good idea – or an extremely good idea – to take action in the garden.

Lunar phase or synodic month

This is the most obvious lunar cycle, the waxing or waning moon. To tell whether the moon is waxing or waning, imagine making a curved shape with your right thumb and index finger, and then your left thumb and index finger. The left hand will make a "C" shape, the right hand an inverted "C." The moon makes the "right hand" inverted "C" shape when waxing and the left hand "C" shape when waning – see Wolf Storl, *Culture and Horticulture*.

Metaphysically, different aspects of life can be said to be emphasized in each quarter. The first quarter, when the moon is growing into a crescent from nothing, is the time for new ideas and expansion: a time of germination. The second quarter, as the moon swells to full, is a time to develop and further expand that which already exists. The full moon signifies completion, so the third quarter is a time when things mature. The fourth quarter, as the crescent moon shrinks away to nothing, is a time of introspection and reflection, preparation for rebirth.

Ascending and descending

These phases are quite different from waxing and waning, and are also known as running high and running low. From the winter solstice to the summer solstice, the constellations that the sun passes through, from Sagittarius to Gemini, have an ascending force, involving expansion, levity, and the energies that cause seed to germinate and plants to rise up out of the ground. From midsummer to midwinter, from Gemini back to Sagittarius, we see descending forces in action. First comes ripening and bearing fruit, then gravity pulls the remains of the plant back down into the earth, and we experience the forces of contraction. The moon expresses this annual expanding-contracting rhythm in miniature every month as it passes through its tour of the zodiac. When the moon is ascending, sap rises, and energy is concentrated on the parts of the plant above ground. When the moon descends, the forces of contraction are stronger, focusing energy on the parts of the plant below ground. Sap retreats downward, aiding the roots.

ABOVE *Nature's annual cycle encompasses the zodiac. From bottom left: the winter snows of Capricorn, Aquarius, and Pisces give way to the spring rains of Aries, Taurus, and Gemini; the summer heat of Cancer, Leo, and Virgo is moderated by the autumn mists of Libra, Scorpio, and Sagittarius.*

Perigee and apogee

The moon's orbital path is elliptical and varies in how near or far away it is from the earth. Perigee (*peri* = nearest, *gaia* = earth) is the closest point, apogee (*apo* = away from) the farthest away. Not surprisingly, the moon's gravitational pull is felt more strongly on earth when the moon is closer to us. Tides run up to a third higher at perigee than they do at apogee.

Sidereal rhythm

Sidereal means time as determined by the movement of the stars. Here, it means the time it takes for the moon to make a tour of the twelve signs of the zodiac and return to its starting place. These moon phases are also very significant for the garden.

LEFT *The almost-full moon's path as it rises above woodland is captured in this stunning time-lapse image, photographed at five-minute intervals. Sowing seed at full moon produces lush growth. Some biodynamists recommend sowing seed two days before a full moon for maximum germination.*

Lunar nodes

This is a wobble. The moon roughly follows the sun's path, known as the ecliptic because eclipses can happen along it, but it actually moves about 5° above or below that path. A moon dipped below the ecliptic is called a descending node; one rising above the ecliptic is an ascending node. Each of these nodes happens once per lunar cycle.

All of these rhythms run close to 27 days, except for the moon phase, which lasts 29.53 days. This makes for a host of interlocking, rarely synchronized cycles. And these variations apply to other planets, too, with the result that the heavens never repeat themselves. Every night the picture in the sky looks different to any other time in the past and it will never occur in exactly the same way again. You can certainly argue for cosmic rhythms here, I think. All these diurnal, seasonal, annual rhythms are pulses, the rhythm of life, that animate us.

Getting started with moonphase gardening

If this is a new way of working in your garden, start gently. Ease yourself into this new way of thinking. Many diaries and calendars show the waxing and waning moon, and there are also specialized biodynamic planting calendars (*see the next chapter*).

Keep your calendar close at hand in the kitchen, or in the garden shed, and refer to it often. Notice where the moon is in its cycle, and begin to be aware of the different effects you may see, feel, or even hear in the garden as the moon waxes and wanes.

Planting

Optimum germination is achieved just before a full moon, which makes this a very good time to sow seeds. This is the sowing time Steiner himself recommends, and was confirmed by the earliest trials of Steiner's *Agriculture* lectures, by Dr Lilly Kolisko, in the 1930s. This is a simple way to begin working with the moon. Dr Kolisko found that sowing two days before a full moon, compared to sowing two days before a new moon, resulted in larger harvests and better growth. Full-moon plants were juicier, and new-moon ones woodier.

Unfortunately, this isn't the whole story. What happens is that seeds absorb most water in the few days before full moon, which is when sap rises most strongly. If you're planting during a time of drought this is undoubtedly the best time to plant. The downside, if there is too much rain, can be lush, soft, leggy growth. Legumes and potatoes will in any case do well at new moon. Peter Proctor, an eminent New Zealand biodynamist, advocates planting when the moon is in opposition to Saturn, i.e. when the two planets are on opposite sides of the earth. He believes that this opposition has a strong balancing effect, resulting in sturdy plants with good fungus resistance. This is one of those times where your common sense comes into play, so that you choose the planting time that's right for your garden and your growing season.

BELOW *Lunar, solar, and planetary paths have been a source of fascination for scientists for many centuries. This 19th-century diagram illustrates the moon's phases as the earth orbits the sun.*

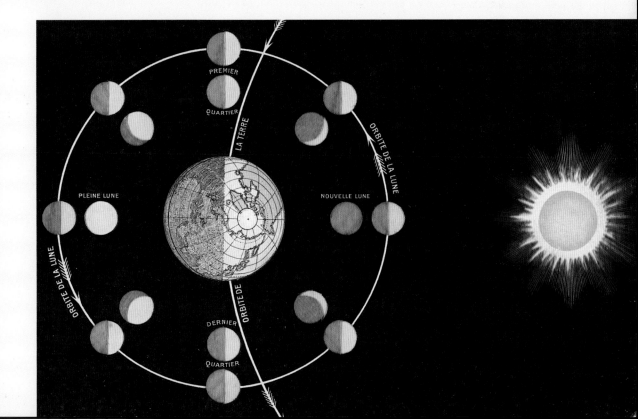

Harnessing the power of the zodiac

Taking account of all the rhythms and cycles of nature is an essential part of biodynamics. It has also been part of mankind's experience and wisdom for centuries. Hippocrates, for example, the ancient Greek philosopher and physician, believed it was foolish to practise medicine without taking into account the movement of the stars. In his theories of science, Hippocrates had no doubt that there were four elements, that were important for understanding both the physical and the metaphysical worlds. Those elements – earth, water, air, and fire/warmth – were central to understanding and maintaining life.

They were linked to different parts of the body, as aids to the diagnosis and treatment of illness; also they were connected to four "humours", or psychological states – melancholic, choleric, phlegmatic, and sanguine – which are still useful as classification tools today. Waldorf schools (*see p.136*) find these distinctions particularly helpful in the guidance and education of children.

The four elements were also assigned qualities that reflected them in nature: earth to weight, water to moisture, air to lightness, and fire to heat. Most of these concepts fell out of use as diagnostic tools when the Age of Enlightenment arrived in the 18th century, yet the four elements still form the basic building blocks of natural science.

Signs and constellations

The sun moves through the 12 signs of the zodiac once every year, and you can observe the different quality the sun has as it moves through each constellation. The fierce Leo sun burning your skin as you pick late-summer crops is much stronger than the late winter sun of Pisces that barely warms the air.

The annual procession that the sun makes through the zodiac is what gives us our sun signs, so that when we say "I'm Sagittarius," for example, we're referring to our sun sign, to the 30-odd days during which the sun passes through that constellation. And we're happy to attribute different qualities to people based on their sun sign, in newspaper astrology columns, for example. I blame my sun sign – Taurus – for my insistent desire to connect with my own patch of earth and scrabble around in it, weeding and pruning and nurturing and observing.

Though these elements may no longer belong to the orthodox scientist's vocabulary, they remain with us through our use of them in the signs of the zodiac. Taurus, Virgo, and Capricorn are earth signs; Cancer, Scorpio, and Pisces are water signs; Gemini, Libra, and Aquarius are air signs; and Aries, Leo, and Sagittarius are classified as fire/warmth signs. This assignment gives each triad of zodiac signs a special connection with one of these four life-forces.

More fours – formative forces

Steiner believes that there are four stages in the formation of plants: first comes the development of the roots, followed by the leaves, as the plant makes its way above the earth; next it flowers, and after flowering it fruits; and the fruit

LEFT *This 15th-century illustration depicts four men purporting to embody the four temperaments, possibly an early attempt at identifying psychological types in order to improve customer relations.*

carries its seeds, through which the next cycle of plant life can begin. Steiner connects an element with each stage of plant growth. Not surprisingly, the earth element works on a plant's roots; the water element works on the leaves; air on the flowers; and the fire/warmth element on the fruit and seeds. I can see a connection to the wateriness of the leaves, the air carrying the perfume many flowers release, and the heat needed to ripen fruit.

Why should plants respond to the planets? Plants have no internal organs as animals or humans do; they cannot move around and forage for food, but are dependent on what they can synthesize from the soil below and the air and water above. The theory goes that the plant's organs are therefore the sun, moon, and stars. For example, the sun provides a daily circulation rhythm for

LEFT *Root vegetables, such as these carrots, are related to the earth signs Taurus, Virgo, and Capricorn (from left to right).*

The four elements

Earth is still the medium in which most plants grow. It holds the minerals and micronutrients that plants need to survive, and is home to the microorganisms that fix necessary nitrogen out of the air. Together clay and humus act like a sponge to absorb water and nutrients. Organic matter, the decaying bodies of plants and animals, is an essential component. Vital soil bacteria and fungi digest this matter and, in the process, release nitrogen.

Water is the medium for carrying nutrients – plant and animal bodies are about 90 percent water. It is the basis of all circulatory systems, whether of a plant, human or planetory.

Air provides the plant's three most important "foods": oxygen, carbon, and nitrogen. Its light forms the opposite pole to earth, which can be said to represent darkness, encouraging the plant upwards from darkness to light. According to Theodor Schwenk, as the plant transpires moisture into the atmosphere, the atmosphere itself forms part of the plant's circulation system. It controls the last stage in the plant's growth cycle: ripening and seeding.

Fire/warmth comes from the sun's light, which provides the warmth everything needs to grow and energy for photosynthesis.

the plant, pulling the sap up in the morning and down again in the afternoon – the daily exhalation and inhalation rhythm. Plants rely on animals to deposit manure and to pollinate them. Deep in the soil, millions of microorganisms live symbiotically around plant roots.

In the 1950s a German biodynamist, Maria Thun (*b.*1922), began to research the potential connection between the four elements of plant formation (*see opposite*) and the four categories of zodiac sign. After 40 years of research, she posits a clear causal relationship between them. Thun categorized plants according

LEFT *Leafy vegetables and salads connect to the water signs Cancer, Scorpio, and Pisces (from left to right).*

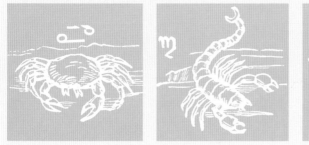

to which part of them we cultivate (*see p.48*). She states that if you attend to your plants during the time when the moon is in the zodiac sign that governs them, you will get better results than if you do not do this. This theory is not in Steiner's original lectures, but an offshoot that has evolved over the years as biodynamists have engaged with the lectures and developed them.

Over the years several researchers have tried to replicate Thun's research – with inconclusive results. Reviewing the research seems to indicate that a quantifiable, if small, improvement in results does follow from using this

LEFT *Flowers thrive under air signs Gemini, Libra, and Aquarius (from left to right).*

calendar. One thing researchers do seem to agree on, however, is that planetary effects are only evident on land farmed organically, and are yet more pronounced on biodynamically cultivated land. Gardens treated with fertilizers and other chemicals apparently show very little response to planetary influences, as if the fertilizers somehow desentize the land so that the soil can no longer respond to these rhythms of nature.

Biodynamics encourages us to use our intention as a positive force in the garden, so it's possible that at least part of the benefits of planting under

Thun's plant groups

Earth = Root vegetables such as beetroot, carrots, garlic, parsnips, and potatoes. In this category are all vegetables whose roots are their most prized feature, even potatoes whose "roots" are really tubers.

Water = All plants prized for their leaves, such as asparagus, cabbage, chicory, grass, kales, Oriental greens, parsley, salad crops, and spinach are in this element.

Air = Flowers: plants whose blossom is most valuable on air days: roses, bulbs, annual and perennial flowers.

Fire/warmth = Fruit and vegetables where we most value the fruit or seed, such as beans, cucumbers, peas, peppers, squashes, tomatoes, and all fruits.

the "right" zodiac influence come from the belief that it *is* the right influence. As you think, so you grow. And any activity, whether it's planting by the planets or using positive intention, that improves the garden is surely worth exploring.

Planting calendars

There is so much information to take into account when working with the planets, and in addition to the zodiac signs there are other planetary aspects that help determine when the cosmos "smiles" upon your garden. The aspects, or angles, that planets make to each other in their ever-unfolding dance can help or hinder garden productivity. The moon's nodes (*see p.38*) are something to avoid and another time not to garden is during solar eclipses. Schwenk, in his book *Sensitive Chaos*, demonstrates that eclipses inhibit seed germination.

Planting calendars have calculated all the possible variants and drawn up a month-by-month scenario illustrating the passage of the waxing and waning moon, the ascending and descending moon, apogee and perigee, and, not least, whether the moon is in an earth, water, air, or fire/warmth zodiac sign. They take into account all the interplay of planetary movements and alignments, weighing up whether these days are good or bad for what needs doing outside.

The first calendar was produced, not surprisingly, by Maria Thun. *Working with the Stars* is a small-format booklet, a translation of the calendar she produces each year in Germany. This calendar is set to Greenwich Mean Time (GMT), but helpfully gives the correct additions and subtractions to make for all other time zones. It leaves users to adjust for British Summer Time by sticking to GMT all year round, allowing for the fact that other countries switch to Daylight Saving Time on different dates.

The second calender on the scene was *Stella Natura*, produced by Sherry Wildfeuer at the Kimberton Hills Camphill Village in Pennsylvania. This is a larger-format calendar, designed to hang on the wall. Each month is accompanied by an article on an aspect of biodynamics and some of these offer very helpful advice. There is also, as in the Thun calendar, a small amount of space allotted each day to record work notes and observations. The calendar is set to Eastern Standard Time and incorporates Daylight Saving Time, but gives no indication of all the adjustments needed for different time zones.

The newest entrant at the time of writing is the *Northern Star* calendar, which has been produced in Australia by Brian Keats using information adjusted to the northern hemisphere from his long-running *Antipodean Astro Calendar*. In full colour, this calendar offers a feast of information, complete with precise details on all the aspects of astronomy that are brought to bear on the decision of when to plant. It is set to Pacific Standard Time. Perhaps the most innovative and useful aspect of Keat's calendar is its visual depiction of the ascending and descending moon. It's easy to monitor moon phases – all we have to do is look up at the moon to see where it is in the phase cycle. It's harder to keep track of ascension and descension, but this calendar makes it easy. All the information is laid out in a gently undulating curve, neatly illustrating the moon's ascending/descending curve. It's like a sinuous sine wave undulating through the year, an elegant visual reminder that all of these cycles really are rhythms.

Interestingly, every year Thun advises that no work should be done in the garden between Good Friday and Easter Sunday, believing that the events that took place on Golgotha more than 2000 years ago had such a profound impact on the planet that their effects can still be felt today. The other two planting calendars reviewed here make no such restriction, however. Keats says, "I think Easter Sunday is a perfectly sublime time for planting." He cautions against treating the calendar as an authority: "I feel quite strongly that calendars can easily become recipe books that seduce people into thinking that biodynamics has all the answers to the correlations of plant rhythms to star and planetary movements. We don't and we have a long journey ahead of us!"

Ordering information for these calendars is given in the Resources directory (*see pp.136–9*). These are by no means the only calendars – some biodynamic associations produce calendars, too; in New Zealand, for example, a NZ calendar is given free to all members – but the three on the previous page are widely available and all you have to do is adjust the times shown to reflect your local time zone; although time-consuming this can be fun to do in the dark winter months when all you've got is the seed catalogues to remind you of warmer times ahead.

So, should you follow a planting calendar? I came across the Thun calendar when I first started learning about biodynamics, before I discovered its evidence was disputed, so I simply incorporated its thinking into my gardening from the beginning. Now, it's force of habit to check the calendar.

I find that working with a calendar also helps me to to overcome procrastination. If I look at the calendar and notice that the only time I can plant out my pot-bound seedlings is in the next two hours otherwise I'll have to force the poor things to wait until the right constellation comes round again, it really motivates me to put my hat on and get outside.

How to use a planting calendar

My advice would be to notice how you feel as you read about using the calendar. If it's something that speaks to you, then go ahead and work with it. If not, you might prefer to start by working with the moon cycles described at the end of the previous chapter and stay with that method until you feel completely comfortable with it. It should bring you good results.

If you decide to take the plunge and plant according to the zodiac, it's worth taking the time to sit down with a garden notebook and plan out exactly when you're going to plant next season's seeds. It'll be helpful if you learn the symbols for the various constellations, too – when I first used a calendar I spent a long time scrabbling around for the key to the symbols, trying to work out what each one meant.

If you start using the calendar once the growing season has begun, however, and your seeds are already in the ground, fear not – simply look at the calendar when you're next heading into the garden, and notice what kind of day it is. If it's a leaf day, weed your lettuces and cabbage; if it's a root day, thin carrots and earth up potatoes. Even watering different plant groups according to the calendar can help them. Any time a plant is handled can have an influence.

Working with a planting calendar has its challenges, but it also has its rewards. You can't work in the garden every day, according to this wisdom. Sometimes there are "blackout days", where planetary influences are so unfavourable, for example when there is an eclipse, that you're advised to do nothing. On such days the only answer is to relax and admire the fruits of your labours.

There's a lot of detail here, and it can be overwhelming to take it all on board at once. What matters more than anything is learning what your patch of land responds to, and developing your intuition. This can be one of the sharpest tools a gardener can use, and it's examined in more detail in Intuitive gardening (*see pp.120–7*). Observing what's actually going on around you, and using common sense, is more important than any calendar. Even if the calendar says a particular time is very favourable for planting, if you go outside and notice a thunderstorm brewing, you don't want to be planting right then.

Have patience, don't try to do it all at once. Gardening is a long-term activity. Do also bear in mind that, although parts of this information have been known and practised for millennia, this is still a new science. Planting rhythms have only been studied and researched for the last 50 or 60 years. We don't have the whole picture yet, which is one of the reasons why there are so many different opinions about the value of planting at different times. What matters is to observe, and to learn from our observations. There's bound to be more to it than we know now.

BELOW *This example of a planting calendar page is taken from Brian Keats'* Northern Star Calendar. *Based in Australia, Keats produces separate calendars for the northern and southern hemispheres. The colour coding and the gentle curves representing the ascending and descending moon's path are easy to follow.*

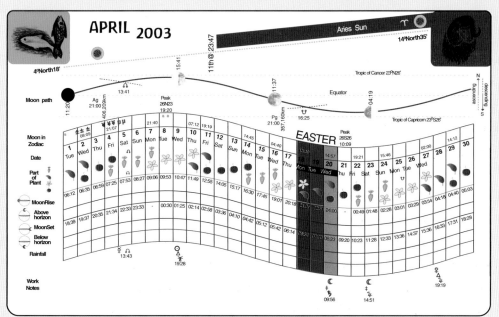

Herbal tonics for your garden

Herbal tonics are nothing new in medicine. I can remember receiving them as a child. Some herbs, such as peppermint, raspberry leaf, and camomile, are widely enjoyed as teas, as much for the taste as for their healing properties.

We've become much more open to the use of herbal remedies again in recent years, perhaps because of an awareness of their often gentle healing properties, with fewer side-effects than laboratory-produced medicines. Enthusiasm for homeopathy, for example, has increased dramatically, as has interest in Chinese herbal medicine.

Twenty years ago I could only obtain Dr Bach flower essences by mail order direct from the producers. A few years later they began to appear in health food stores. Now they're advertized on the London Underground and sold in numerous pharmacies.

Of course you can use any preparation you like on your garden. For instance, I happen to like adding Dr Bach's Rescue Remedy, described as an all-purpose comforter, to plants I think might be shocked or distressed. I also add a drop of Walnut (Bach's essence offering protection from powerful influences) to support plants I've just transplanted.

I see nothing wrong with using whatever substances you think will help your garden – provided they're not toxic chemicals. In the following chapters, however, I'm going to focus on the nine preparations Rudolf Steiner recommended, all of which are designed to help your garden heal. It has to be said that some of these suggestions sound bizarre, even like hocus-pocus. A freshly-butchered cow skull? Animal intestines? Awfully close to *eye of newt and toe of frog and fire burn and cauldron bubble.*

But stay with me, for I wish to show that at no point does Steiner expect us to follow his guidance blindly. He has a logical reason for everything he suggests. You could see it as being scientific in a holistic sense, tapping into the connections between science and folk wisdom and metaphysics, and fusing these elements to come up with something that may appear ridiculous but does, in fact, contain a deep and persuasive logic.

In the biodynamic world-view nothing happens in isolation. A sick plant, for example, should not be seen as an isolated incident but as a symptom that something is wrong in the plant's environment. A plant is not just leaves, stem, and roots but an entity directly bound up with everything that happens in its habitat and affected by what's going on in each of the four elements – earth, water, air, and fire/warmth. That means that a soil poisoned by insecticides will have influence on a plant. Chemical residues in the groundwater will find their way into plant cells. Blazing heat can scorch leaves. Very wet conditions, or overwatering, can cause fungal attack. The list is endless and infinitely varied.

Just as human organisms turn to herbal teas or flower essences to correct internal imbalances, so gardeners can use specially treated animal, vegetable, or mineral substances to correct plant imbalances. And in the same way that many humans favour plant remedies over chemically created ones for slower,

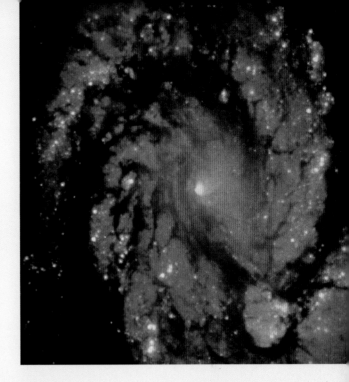

gentler effects, so biodynamic remedies work more gently on the soil and the plant than quick chemical fixes.

These remedies will benefit the garden in various ways. The first, most urgent need, of course, is to use them to help heal soil that has been abused by chemicals, even soil damaged over the course of many years. Then, once the soil has restored health and vitality, continuing to use the remedies will keep it in optimum condition, year after year. Certain remedies can also be used to deal with specific garden problems such as fungal attacks.

ABOVE *This Hubble photograph of the M1000 spiral galaxy clearly shows the spiral nature of its formation, an arrangement reflected and repeated in microcosms throughout nature.*

The idea, metaphysically speaking, is that these remedies act as a wake-up call, opening up the soil to sensitize it, enabling it to interact with and utilize the cosmic forces streaming in. These energies are zooming around all the time, but the soil isn't necessarily receptive to them. It's like radio waves that bounce around at every moment, but, unless the radio is turned on and tuned to the right station, we're oblivious to the information being sent.

Two of these remedies, the first two (*see pp.56–7*), are intended for direct application in the garden. Another seven are designed to be added indirectly, via the compost pile that then turns to humus and is fed to the soil. The final remedy is designed to combat fungal problems. The compost and fungal remedies will be dealt with in later chapters. The remedies, commonly known as "preps," for preparations, were given these numbers by the experimental farming group that began working on Steiner's suggestions after his death. This group also gave the name "biodynamic" to the agricultural system that emerged from Steiner's lectures.

There are two stages to using the remedies: first, making them and then, secondly, preparing them for use. In the case of the first two, preparation for use involves stirring them in water using a special method. It isn't essential to be able to make the preps yourself, because they are available ready-made; it is, however, a must to prepare them for use yourself, and the basic method for doing that will be explained first, followed by a description of what each prep contains and how it's made.

Homeopathy

The law of similars was known to Hippocrates and used in many ancient cultures, from the Mayans and Chinese to Native Americans. This law states that like can be treated with like, meaning that a substance that induces disease in a healthy person can be used to cure a similar disease occurring in a sick person. A German doctor, Samuel Hahnemann (1755–1843), created a systematic science from the law of similars in the late 18th century and called it homeopathy. Homeopathy rapidly gained mainstream acceptance in Europe and America by the late 19th century, and its popularity alarmed doctors of what is now thought of as orthodox medicine. (Hahnemann coined the term "allopath," meaning the treatment of disease by inducing an opposite condition.) It has even been suggested that the American Medical Association was formed by a group of doctors of Western medicine who were concerned that homeopathy threatened their business.

Homeopathy looks at a person as a whole unit, body and mind and spirit, and seeks to heal the whole person rather than a collection of symptoms. Biodynamics does the same when it steps back to gain a holistic view of all the forces working on a garden, from cosmic forces from above to the bacteria buried in the soil. Biodynamics uses the preparations homeopathically, treating like with like, but instead using disease-inducing substances it uses substances that encourage growth, inoculating the soil with these positive forces.

Just like biodynamics, homeopathy draws on a variety of substances, mostly vegetable and mineral, with a few animal. The key to homeopathic remedy preparation is potentizing. This involves progressive dilution of the basic healing substance in water. In homeopathy the dynamizing, potentizing act is called succussion – the repeated shaking and striking of the vessel containing the remedy against a hard but giving surface, such as a paperback book or your hand.

The first two biodynamic preparations – the "horn preps"

The first two remedies form opposite ends of a polarity, like hot and cold, positive and negative. The reason they are sometimes called the "horn preps" is that they are stuffed into a cow's horn before burial. According to Steiner, horns are natural receptacles for cosmic forces, focusing and concentrating these forces into the biodynamic preparations contained within them during their long burial period. Steiner also said that hooves work just as well, but most prep-makers use horns.

Horn Dung or Horn Manure, preparation 500, works on the earth, encouraging expansion and levity, promoting germination, and assisting microorganism growth in the soil and root growth in the plant. Horn Manure will also regulate lime and nitrogen content and aid the release of trace elements. It is the foundation remedy, supporting all the work that will be done in the future.

Horn Quartz or Horn Silica, preparation 501, works in the atmosphere above the soil, assisting fruiting and flowering, maturation, and contraction.

Horn Quartz is a growth stimulant that will transmit the forces of light and warmth, sensitize the garden, and open it up to receive the forces streaming in from the cosmos. It enhances the plant's ability to metabolize light, stimulates photosynthesis and the formation of chlorophyll, and can also increase resistance to disease and insects. In addition, it is influential in improving the taste and nutritional value of what you grow as well as its longevity.

Dynamizing the biodynamic preparations

This is one of the most crucial parts of the process. It involves stirring a tiny amount of a preparation in a bucket or barrel for an hour. The purpose of stirring is to create a vortex. Through the vortex the maximum amount of water will be exposed to the air and through the air, to the forces of the cosmos. The repeated stirring and the creation of the resulting deep vortexes opens up a greater surface area of water than a still surface and gives the cosmic forces more opportunity to interact with the water and impart their forces to it – in other words, to dynamize it. The spiral-shaped vortex reflects the shape of the cosmos itself, as the deep-space photographs from the Hubble telescope show (*see p.55*), and, as Schwenk points out, the movement of water in a vortex – fast at the centre, slower at the periphery – mirrors the orbit of planets around the sun. Planets close to the sun make their transits much faster than those further away.

LEFT *A collection of cow horns stuffed with manure, awaiting overwinter burial. In a form of alchemy these horns, will yield sweet-smelling, crumbly compost the following spring, ready to be diluted, dynamized, and sprayed on the waiting ground.*

How to dynamize

Empty a pinch of your chosen prep into a bucket of rainwater and stir vigorously with a circular motion until there is a crater in the water reaching almost to the bottom of the bucket. Take out the stirring implement, pause for a few seconds, and then plunge the stick or your arm back in, and stir the other way with equal vigour. The water seethes and tumbles each time you change direction, bursting with energy like it's leaping down rocks or spurting from a dam. The point is to create chaos each time you change direction, then give the water a new pattern, and then create chaos again. Keep this up for an hour and just watch what happens. You may notice that the water seems to change consistency, becoming more viscous. Stirring opens up the surface of the water to the air and the cosmic forces, enlivening it.

I don't think this task is as tiring as stirring a cake mix for an hour. Maybe it's that tiny pause in between changing vortex directions that gives me the rest I need, but I prefer to think that it's because it's a more profound activity than making cakes (though who's to say a sponge doesn't have its place in the spiritual realms as well?). I always seem to pause, mentally, when watching the vortex spin for a second or two, before I create chaos and move the stick the other way. It draws me in, becomes like a meditation, and has a very calming influence.

Watch, listen, sense, feel; be aware of how the water is changing during the preparation process. In my experience, it feels as though the water becomes thicker. It's almost like kneading dough; you just know there's a moment when the bread changes consistency as the yeast works, and you know the bread is ready to be set aside to prove.

How long does it take?

An hour is long enough to fully dynamize the mixture. After you've gone through this a few times you'll probably begin to be able to sense when the water is "done" without looking at the clock. Just like knowing when that kneaded loaf is ready to prove, you may find after a while that you become very aware of when this shift happens. Until you do, don't worry. Just notice the time, and stay focused on what you are doing. Stirring makes you part of the process at a very fundamental level. Repeated sessions will certainly enhance your awareness.

It's a simple process, yet one that can have profound effects. Perhaps that's why so many orthodoxies have arisen around what and how it should be done, especially concerning the stirring action. There are several variables here. Some people stir by hand, some use a stick, and others prefer a bunch of birch twigs. I have heard biodynamic gardeners spend all evening arguing about whether stirring should begin from the edge of the barrel moving towards the centre, or start at the centre working towards the outside – or whether the first vortex spiral should be clockwise or anti-clockwise.

The first time this was ever done, under the supervision of Steiner, the stirring implement used was a walking stick belonging to one of the participants – hardly a mystical choice. Nor was there any mention of clockwise versus anti-clockwise, nor of whether to start in the centre or at the edge. These are all things that people have experimented with afterwards and drawn their own conclusions about.

I don't believe there is one right way. I've stirred with a stick and with my hand. I've even stirred a full rain-barrel, enough for an 8-ha (20-acre) farm, using my whole arm, and really enjoyed getting stuck in. One of the key factors is the frame of mind you are in when you approach the task – what is often called "intention". I think it's better to stir for an hour with whatever is to hand, and to be completely present and mindful of the task you're undertaking; this is not something that's always easy to do, given the hectic pace of life most of us endure. Stirring offers a rare opportunity to stop and really pay attention.

ABOVE Do not let this drawing deceive you – it really isn't necessary to stir the preps with nothing on, in fact I would definitely not recommend it. If kneeling isn't comfortable, get a chair and lean over the vessel, resting your elbows on your knees.

Spraying

As soon as the stirring is finished, the solution needs to be put to use as it won't keep for more than an hour. Carry a bowl or bucket of stirred prep and walk the garden, dispensing it in an arc over the entire garden, using big drops for 500 and a fine mist for 501. No need to stick to just one patch of the garden, such as the vegetable plot, because the whole area will benefit. Work out a route that takes in the perimeter of the property, followed by a strip-by-strip approach so that the whole garden is covered. It isn't necessary to spray every centimetre, because it's not about saturating the ground with liquid. The whole garden is influenced by the prep whether or not it has directly received a droplet.

Using 500

One purchased unit of 500, or 25g (1oz), will cover up to 0.4ha (1 acre) of garden, which should be more than enough for most needs. If neighbours show an interest, get together to stir and then give everyone a portion to spray on their garden. Steiner felt that applying 500 would make an excellent activity – he suggested stirring after Sunday lunch.

Timing

The best time of day to spray 500 is late afternoon or early evening, with the earth's contracting rhythm (which begins at 3pm), so that the soil draws the preparation into itself. An ideal moment to do this is with the evening dew. Actually, "spray" is a slight misnomer for 500; flicking a big brush, such as a new paintbrush, or a bunch of twigs dipped in the liquid, is the best way to apply this prep. If you use a handsprayer, make sure it's set to spray large droplets rather than a fine mist.

Watch the weather. Avoid spraying immediately before or after rain, during high winds (the prep will be blown away), or in strong sun, which will provoke premature evaporation. Make sure that the soil itself is not waterlogged, nor

BELOW *Nature's cosmic spiral reveals itself again, here at the top of a water vortex, perfect in proportion and power. This is the shape to recreate when stirring the preps in a water bucket.*

too dry for planting. Ideally, allow enough daylight time after spraying to work the planting beds over lightly with a fork or hoe, to incorporate the 500 into the soil so that it can begin its work.

How often should I do this?

Again, experts differ in their opinions about exactly when this should happen, but I think that several times a year is pretty much essential. Use the prep in the autumn, before the soil freezes, to support the soil during the winter when it becomes most alive (*see p.33 for more information on the soil in winter*). Then at the start of spring spray once the soil has thawed, and again later in spring if there has been drought, or on plants damaged by frost or wind.

That's the traditional approach. Alternatively, take a more individualized view, spraying small areas of soil before planting each new bed and into the planting hole before transplanting. Again, this is one of those areas where personal preference comes into play. Spraying several times a year gives the garden the basic wake-up call it needs, but go on to experiment by adding additional specific sprayings to particular crops, and see whether you like the results.

ABOVE *In this side view of a water vortex, the spiral reaches deep into the water, lifting up and incorporating water in its action all the way down, deep into the bucket.*

Using 501

Take a pinch, no more than a gram, and dynamize it in a 14l (3 gallon) bucket of rainwater, as for the Horn Manure preparation (500). Warm the water to room temperature if possible. Preparation 501 is mostly used as a foliar spray. Its action stimulates above- rather than below-ground growth – so use it on the leaves, flowers, and immature fruits. A fine mist is best, rather than the large droplets of 500 that fall from a brush or bunch of twigs. A small handspray pump is ideal, or even a mister of the sort hairdressers use for dampening hair.

When to apply 501

Spray first thing in the morning, at dawn or soon after, as soon as the dew has evaporated, to catch the upward-moving forces working in the plants. It can be very effective to spray 500 one evening and 501 the following morning. They

are, after all, a complementary pair of remedies, and it seems sensible to use them in swift succession, so that the garden hears your wake-up call. Both of these solutions will have most effect if used after the soil has received compost treated with the compost preps, or barrel compost (*see pp.75–6*); in fact many people say that there won't be much benefit from 500 and 501 unless the soil has first received the other preps, through biodynamic compost or one of its equivalents.

It is interesting here to quote first-time stirrer, Bonnie York: "When stirring the 501, the water seemed almost fluffy. It was very light and felt 'frothy' in comparison to the 500. All in all, it was a wonderful experience."

Flowforms

Stirring by hand is the simplest way to dynamize, and one that works satisfactorily for most domestic gardens and small farms. In countries such as Australia, however, where farms of hundreds of hectares are common, stirring by hand is not practicable, and some very ingenious experiments have been made with stirring machines.

By far the most aesthetically pleasing of these is the flowform, created by John Wilkes, a British sculptor and biodynamist. Flowforms most commonly consist of a series of basins. Water is pumped to the top of the basins and then gradually cascades down through them. The basins are artfully designed to hold the water for a while and send it into a lemniscate, or figure-of-eight pattern, so that the water gradually takes on a pulsing rhythm. The figure-of-eight patterns create the vortexes that are needed for the dynamizing process. The clockwise and anti-clockwise vortexes are set up by the pulsing of the water through the basins, which even creates the necessary "chaos" moment in between. I find this absolutely mesmerizing to watch and can sit by a flowform for hours, completely entranced by the unfolding patterns.

How 500 and 501 are made

500: In autumn, fresh cow manure is packed into a cow horn and buried in the garden over winter, to absorb the soil's vitality and life-force at the time of year when it is most alive. The horns are dug up again in late spring, sometime after Easter, by which time the smelly manure is transformed into beautiful, friable, pleasant-smelling humus.

501: Finely ground quartz crystal is transformed into a paste by being mixed with rainwater, and then stuffed into a cow horn. Preparation 501 is made in the spring, so that the horn lies in the warm soil over the summer and absorbs light and heat; it is dug up again in the autumn.

Can horns be recycled? Certainly. They should last for three or four burials before they lose their efficacy.

Getting hold of the preps

The easiest way to get started with the preps is simply to buy them by mail order. The national biodynamic associations have plenty of information available to the public on reliable prep-making sources. (*Addresses are given on page 138*.)

Of course, this isn't the ideal solution. Biodynamics is, after all, about a personal connection with the land, and preps imported from another part of the country can't forge as close a connection with your patch as the ones you make in your own garden.

The cow

What's the importance of the cow for this process? Both cow dung and a cow's horn are called for – not just any old horn, either, but preferably one from an animal that has borne several calves, lived a long, healthy life, and died of old age rather than of disease. It's hard to find a source for horns in these days of routine de-horning, so a local biodynamic society may be a good source of information and assistance (*see p.138*). (Note that you can also use a cow's hoof for the burial process.)

I think that there is something of the nature of the cow involved here. A holy animal in India, the cow is a ruminant, which means an animal that chews the cud, re-digesting its food through its four stomachs. Ruminant has given us the verb "to ruminate," meaning to meditate, to ponder. The cow is so well-known as a placid, peaceful animal that we hardly give it a second thought, but perhaps what it is doing as it ruminates is interacting repeatedly with the forces of the plant matter it is digesting.

But it's not necessarily easy making your own preps when you're just getting started. My advice at the beginning would be to make this a two-stage learning process, the first step being to join a prep-making workshop. Many local biodynamic societies get together each year to make enough preps for all members to use. This can be a fun way of getting started, as you may meet some like-minded people, tap into useful networks for answering specific questions, and learn more about the best way of coping with local conditions. Months later you'll come away with preps you have a direct connection to because you've helped create them. And you'll have seen and experienced at first hand how these complex-sounding procedures actually work in practice.

Armed with that knowledge, perhaps you can go ahead the next year and source a couple of mature cow horns and bury your own 500 and 501, because there's no doubt about it: the best preps for your garden are the ones created within it.

Storing the preps

It's important to preserve the energies within the preps. The horns can be left in the ground until their contents are needed, but once dug up the contents can be stored in a wooden box loosely filled with moist earth or peat moss. They have as much need for care as freshly-harvested vegetables, and it's preferable to keep them in natural materials such as clay or glass rather than plastics.

The most important thing is to stop your preps drying out, while still allowing them to breathe. Glass jars or ceramic pots are best to achieve this, but don't screw the lids on tight – allow a little ventilation. They are best stored in

the dark with the exception of 501 – this is happy basking in the sun and is best kept on a windowsill in a clear-glass container with a glass or metal lid.

A popular method is to pack the prep-filled pots in several centimetres (inches) of moist earth or peat moss inside another container, such as a crate or wooden box. It's certainly a good idea to keep them all together. Store the box in a cool dark place, but make sure it doesn't freeze and keep it well away from pungent-smelling chemicals.

Biodynamic composting

The organic gardening movement has done a wonderful job of showing gardeners that they have the means right on their doorsteps of creating all the food their garden requires, without reaching for artificial fertilizers.

Water-soluble fertilizers out of a packet over-accelerate a plant's growth, leading to lush, distended stems that are weak and prone to disease. Not only that, they can flush through the soil and into the groundwater, causing a chain of pollution problems. It's not the answer for the garden or the planet.

Soil that has had chemicals pumped into it over the years is inert and lifeless. Plants growing in this inert soil have to be fed soluble inputs in order to grow. Organic gardening takes the opposite view: feed the soil, and the soil itself will feed the plants.

Biodynamics takes this a step further. Harking back to the initial impetus of creating biodynamics – to provide tools to heal an earth weakened by intensive chemical farming – it uses a range of herbal remedies directly in the compost pile in order to boost the effectiveness of the compost. There are various ways of doing this. I'll start by explaining the "classic" biodynamic method, which requires quite a lot of space and compostable materials, and then look at simple ways of adapting this method for use in smaller gardens.

Biodynamic compost is remarkable stuff. It improves tilth, the soil's overall condition and friability, so that early crops can be planted even earlier in the spring. Compost alters humus content for the better, and humus retains water, so the soil both needs less water and retains what is does have for longer. It deepens the soil's colour, and darker-coloured soils will retain more of the sun's precious heat so that the soil warms up earlier in the season – another good way of getting an early start in terms of growing. This same principle extends the growing season further into autumn.

Compost also attracts earthworms, part of the soil's life-force, into the soil. Adding compost to sandy soil will improve its retentiveness and absorption, so it will hold water better. Compost will also change the texture of clay soils, giving them an easily worked crumbly texture.

Compost ingredients

First of all, though, what can be composted? Almost anything organic, would be the short answer, right down to the contents of the vacuum-cleaner bag. The key to building a good compost heap is diversity. Many people don't recommend the use of cooked kitchen scraps, but when I worked on a community farm we composted everything except food that had come into contact with vinegar. We even, I discovered, tried to compost the odd fork that had been accidentally thrown into the slops pail, and these – plus meat bones – were about the only thing that refused to succumb to the compost process. Six months after building this putrid, smelly pile we were forking off quantities of rich crumbly brown humus – sweet-smelling and the best possible nourishment for a garden. It's alchemy again – turning base materials into green gold.

We were lucky not to be troubled by dogs or rats. If that is the case it may be preferable to compost kitchen scraps in a wormery – the special kind of worms needed for this, *Eisenia foetida*, are available by mail order. They're smaller than compost piles, so they're suitable for small gardens, and they can be kept close to the kitchen for convenience, if you can stand the smell.

I'm a great enthusiast for slinging as much material onto the pile as possible, though I don't use the roots of pernicious weeds such as couch grass. There are ways to deal with these roots to render them harmless for composting but at this point I decide that yes, I admit it, life's too short, and I throw them in the dustbin, or burn them.

ABOVE *How long a compost heap takes to perform its alchemy on your garden waste depends on many factors, particularly temperature and rainfall. Check your heap regularly: water it if it is drying out, protect it if it's becoming waterlogged.*

I do draw the line at pet faeces, too, though there are those who are in favour of it. I want to be certain that no viruses are passed on. I know that many viruses are destroyed in the heat that builds up in the compost pile but, especially if there are children around, I simply don't care to risk it.

Lawn clippings are fine for a compost heap, but I would encourage you to consider planting something else to replace your lawn, if you can bear it. Lawns are such sponges for water that some drought-ridden parts of the USA are now paying gardeners to dig up their lawns and plant drought-resistant shrubs instead. And think of all that productive extra space for crops such as apples, raspberries, and asparagus.

Compost sites

Where should the pile be built? In a small garden there may not be much choice of site, but if possible opt for a shady area preferably under a broad-leaved tree. Avoid trees with invasive roots, or with needles that are hard to digest. Birch, elder, alder, and hazelnut seem to have a particular affinity for compost piles; if you're fortunate enough to have one of these trees in your garden, building a compost heap beneath would be ideal.

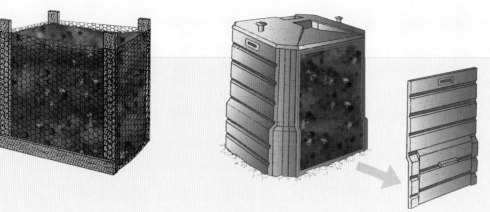

The pile will need protecting from the wind, so bear that in mind when siting the structure. Also make sure that the heap is accessible and the path wide enough to accommodate a wheelbarrow; if the pile is close to the kitchen it's easier to deposit the waste every day. The hose needs to reach it, too.

The classic biodynamic compost heap consists of a fairly big pile, or windrow, 1.5m (5ft) wide and as tall as you have materials for and space allows. Domestic gardeners are not in that league, but start gathering plenty of different materials right away in order to get the heap going as soon as the structure is complete. (If you haven't much in the way of compost materials and can only add to the pile a little at a time, don't worry; there's a way of dealing with this that I'll come to shortly.)

You need to aim for a minimum of 1 cub m (35 cub ft) in volume, more if you have room in the garden and can find enough raw materials to sustain it. Garden centres and seed catalogues have a reasonable selection of composting containers – look for ones that provide aeration spaces and are base-less, i.e. open to the ground – or you can build your own. I've seen all manner of ingeniously built compost containers, often made from recycled materials. Old fork-lift pallets are ideal; the slats are just the right length. And chicken wire is excellent to use for the inner support.

So, gather your ingredients. A mix that will, ideally, balance "brown stuff" and "green stuff" to give an equal balance of carbon and nitrogen. Carbon-rich "brown stuff" includes straw, used mulch, spent hops, dry leaves, and old hay. Nitrogen-rich "green stuff" includes outer vegetable leaves, grass clippings, weeds and manure, plus honorary materials such as coffee grounds. Then you'll need some rock powders: powdered limestone is good and granite dust or greensand are also recommended.

What about manure? Cows play a major role in Steiner's ideal farm model, but obviously most gardeners have neither the time nor space, to say nothing of the inclination, to keep livestock. Animal manures can be obtained in a variety of different ways (*see pp.76 and 77*). If none of these are available, urine makes a good source of nitrogen; mix one part urine with three parts water and applied straight to the pile when building.

Building the compost pile

First of all, fork over the ground where you'll build the pile. You want soil organisms to have access, so build the pile directly on the earth – don't put any protective layer down first. Spray some fresh 500 (*see pp.56–65*) on the ground if it is available and then start the pile with thick plant stalks. These stalks will take a while to break down but it'll give a little space at the bottom for air.

Build the pile with alternating green and brown layers. Now is the time to add another key element – water. It really is surprising how much water a compost pile needs to get going. Everything in the heap must be thoroughly moistened. Straw or autumn leaves, for instance, should be soaked before using so that they take on the consistency of a wrung-out sponge.

After a green layer, sprinkle on a thin layer of earth. This acts as a kind of "starter," an inoculant for the soil organisms that play such a large part in breaking the compost down. The earth will also trap any ammonia given off by the green matter as it breaks down. Lightly spray each layer of earth with some more 500.

Adding Steiner's remedies to the compost pile

In the case of a large heap that has been built in one go, add the remedies once the pile is complete. If the heap it to be constructed a little at a time, however, put them in when the pile is about half finished. Make six evenly spaced holes, about 50cm (20in) deep, each pointing towards heart of the heap. I use the blunt end of a rake or hoe, a long-handled trowel, or even a stick, for this. Take a portion of 502, roll it into a little ball, and post it down the hole, gently tapping it down to the bottom with your stick. Repeat this procedure with 503, 504, 505, and 506 (*see p.79*). Next fill each hole with compost, preferably mature, and tamp it down firmly so thatthe prep ball sits in direct contact with its surroundings rather than an air pocket.

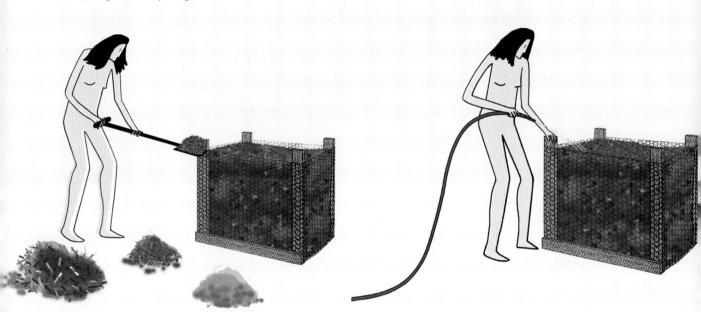

Now add 507, the valerian solution, to 4.5l (1gal) of rainwater and dynamize it for five minutes. Pour half of this solution down the last remaining hole, then put the rest into a watering can and spray it over the whole heap.

ABOVE *Add your green stuff and brown stuff to the pile in layers. Wet it thoroughly, until the mix feels like a wrung-out sponge, then cover the top if it looks like it is going to rain.*

The compost pile and the four elements

Compost needs the action of all four elements – earth, air, water, and fire/warmth – to help its raw materials transform into effective humus. Earth isn't just a necessary component inside the compost pile. A good pile also needs a protective skin, just like the earth's crust, so build a protective layer over the pile to act as the skin. Straw is good.

Water isn't only important when building the pile. If it's very rainy, cover the top of the heap with tarpaulin, or even a piece of old carpet. If it's dry, monitor the pile for evaporation and add water if it seems in danger of drying out. Burrow into it from time to time to check on the moisture content, the pile should not be wringing wet nor bone dry. Fill the hole in afterwards.

Another advantage of keeping the pile moist is that it will encourage any weed seeds to germinat and then die; this ensures that they aren't around to germinate when the compost is spread on the garden.

It is not necessary to turn this pile to aerate it. There are many organic advocates of turning, but if it has been built correctly in the first place, you can just sit back and let it do its work.

Fire/warmth comes into play as the decomposition processes start to work and the pile heats up. It'll reach a peak heat of up to 80°C (176°F) then settle back to a somewhat cooler temperature, at which point the earthworms should start moving in to help the whole composting process.

The compost pile will be ready between four and eight months after it has been built. No two heaps are alike – they almost seem to have a life of their own, depending on weather and other conditions – but, roughly speaking, a pile built in spring will be ready in autumn, and a pile built in early autumn will be ready the following spring. The pile will sink to nearly half its size, but when it is uncovered, you'll find a heap of the most wonderful ripe humus, ready to work its miracle on your garden.

When to use the compost

It may come as a surprise, especially if you have made and used compost by organic methods, that far less compost is needed than in organic gardening. In the first year use 1l per 0.4sq m (0.22gal per 4sq ft), reducing that to 1l per 0.5sq m (0.22gal per 6sq ft) each year thereafter. Work it into the soil immediately, rather than leaving it on the surface where it might blow away. It needs to interact with the soil to have an effect. By the second year you'll see an improvement; by the third year you should notice a big difference.

The difference the preps make

The effects of the preps were researched by the United States Department of Agriculture (USDA), in 1999. Their researchers found that "use of the biodynamic compost preparations could speed the composting process, better destroy pathogens and weed seeds in the material by maintaining high temperatures longer, and change the value of the resulting compost as a fertilizer by increasing the amount of nitrate." (*See Resources Directory, page 138.*)

Two shortcuts for small gardens

There's no shortcut to using the herbal preparations – the influence of those preps is needed on the garden; the only question is, how best to do it. Luckily, there are some shortcuts with part of this. Some of the early biodynamic pioneers recognized the need for methods that would help people get started quickly instead of them having to wait months for the compost pile to mature.

1. Pfeiffer Compost Starter

Ehrenfried Pfeiffer (1899–1961), a microbiologist and one of Steiner's first students, brought biodynamics to the USA. One of his great initiatives was to develop what he called a Compost Starter, which is a compost inoculant. It is designed to inoculate the compost with a variety of different microorganisms, as well as small quantities of the compost preps. Unfortunately, the Pfeiffer Compost Starter isn't available everywhere. If you can get hold of it you will find it a valuable shortcut to help you get started; if you can't, try the second shortcut, Barrel Compost (*see next page*).

If you use this starter, you don't even have to add animal manure to the compost pile. It is ideal when you only have a small amount of compostable material available in your garden and can therefore only build a small pile.

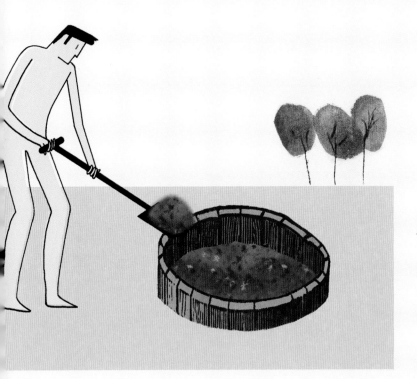

LEFT *To make Maria Thun's Barrel Compost first turn the mixture over and over with spades for an hour, making sure all the ingredients are thoroughly mixed together. Next fill the container that has been sunk into the ground with the mixture.*

2. Barrel Compost

Biodynamics researcher Maria Thun created a particularly useful way of getting the beneficial effects of the compost preparations onto your land in just a couple of months. This concoction has been known by at least half a dozen nicknames, including Barrel Compost, the Compost Preparation, Barrel Preparation, Cowpat Pit, and Cowpat Preparation. It's not difficult to guess what the main ingredient is.

To make this preparation take 50l (11gal) of fresh cow dung (that's about five buckets), 100g (4oz) of crushed eggshells from uncooked eggs (organic for preference, of course, but free range at the very least), and 500g (18oz) of finely ground basalt sand.

Find some space in the garden with a hard surface and dump the dung on the ground, sprinkle onto it the basalt and eggshells; next take a spade and "stir" it for an hour. In practice, this means cutting and shovelling the dung; lifting a spadeful and turning it over. I have found this is very good work to do in a group of three or four. Each participant takes a spade and walks slowly round the pile, shovelling and turning as they go. Many hands do make lighter, or at least more companionable, work. It's interesting to see how different the well-stirred mixture looks from to the initial ingredients.

Now take the dung and place it in a rudimentary box that you've half-buried in the ground. The original "recipe" called for a half-barrel, without its lid, that was buried half in and half out of the ground, to a depth of up to 0.6m (2ft). Again, no bottom is needed on the barrel because the soil beneath needs to interact with the mixture that's going to be buried. A curved barrel is nice, but a rectangular wood frame will work just as well; make it about 0.2sq m (2sq ft), and use wood that hasn't been painted or treated.

Bury half the mixture in the barrel or frame and add a half portion of each compost preparation, 500 or 501, (a portion being the unit you buy from a biodynamic association). Insert each preparation individually, as for the instructions for the compost heap (see p.71). Then put in the remaining mixture, followed by the remaining preps.

The final stage is to stir five drops of valerian in 1l (0.22gal) of water for 15 minutes. Pour the dynamized liquid over the mixture, then cover the container with a wooden lid – a board will do. Leave it for a month, then open it up, and stir it round before covering it up again and leaving it for another two to four weeks.

Now it's ready for use. Take 25g (1oz) and stir it into a bucket of water for an hour, creating vortexes both clockwise and anti-clockwise as with dynamizing 500 and 501. Spray it on the garden immediately, in late afternoon.

Alternatives to cow manure

Not everyone can lay their hands, so to speak, on good-quality cow manure. If it isn't available, there are other options. I'm indebted to Dave Robison of the Oregon biodynamic group for some of the following suggestions.

Chicken waste

Although chicken waste has a high ammonia content, those who keep chickens, or know someone who does, will find that the compost pile is the perfect way to recycle the chicken waste. Chickens will also provide a constant source of eggshells for making Barrel Compost.

Rabbit droppings

If you happen to know a local family whose children keep rabbits you could always try to "Adopt-A-Bunny," and take the droppings off their hands.

Horse manure

As a child I lived near a beach, and every evening the donkeys who had spent the day on the sands giving rides would trot back up our street to their stables. Every evening my grandfather would keep an eye out, and scoot into the road with a shovel if any of the donkeys left a deposit. Later, I lived near a riding stables, and every weekend similar natural resources would be lying in the road after the ride had gone by. Horse manure can work very well in a compost pile, and there may well be a farm or stables not too far from you that doesn't use chemical inputs and would be happy to let you take away the relatively small quantity needed.

A word of warning to all those who collect stable manure from commercial establishments: beware of straw. Certain herbicides in use at the time of writing will not break down in the compost pile. Commercially bought hay and straw may have had such herbicides applied, and adding these to the heap could result in poisoned compost. To be on the safe side I'd suggest avoiding stable bedding unless you can be sure of the source. Also avoid horse bedding made from cedar chips.

Commercial cow manure

Yes, this may well contain antibiotics, but in small amounts these are most likely to break down in the composting process. Be cautious about straw, for the reason explained above.

Zoo poo

In some cities zoo keepers are enlightened enough to make available to the public the manure their charges produce. This opens up a whole new ball game. Elephants? Yes, they're herbivores, not ruminants like cows, but with a strong digestive process. Llamas and antelopes produce dung similar to that of sheep or goats.

Worms

Wormeries have been mentioned before (*see p.69*), and I do think for the urban garden they're ideal. Compact, low maintenance, and voracious, worms eat their own weight daily. To avoid attracting rats or dogs, you need to set up an enclosed wormery.

RIGHT AND BELOW
Three of the plants Rudolf Steiner recommends using for healing the soil: valerian (top), camomile (left), and nettle (right). Using plants that grow like weeds in Europe is perfect utilization of natural resources. Biodynamic gardeners in parts of the world where these plants are not indigenous are experimenting to see whether local plants offer effective substitutes.

Herbal remedies:the compost preps

The use of earth in the compost pile is a biodynamic innovation, as is the addition of rock powders. The key difference between organic and biodynamic composting lies, though, in the use of specific herbal remedies. All the herbs Steiner indicated here as preparations were already widely known in herbal lore as being of medicinal value, and in some ancient systems of wisdom they were also assigned to different planets. Some people in biodynamics feel that each preparation is linked to a different planet, and brings into the garden the forces associated with that planet. In this theory, 502 is linked with the planet Venus, 503 with Mercury, 504 with the sun or Mars, 505 with the moon, 506 with Jupiter, and 507 with Mars or Saturn.

*Yarrow blossoms (*Achillea millefolium*) – Preparation 502*

Yarrow is connected with potassium and sulphur and is said to bring the forces of light into the soil. Its purpose is to help plants attract trace elements and optimize their nutritional uptake. Yarrow blossoms are stuffed into a deer, stag, or hart bladder, which is hung up in sunlight during the summer, then cut down in the autumn and buried in fertile soil over winter. By the time it is dug up the following summer it has had a full year of atmospheric and subterranean forces working on it. Perhaps it isn't too fanciful to see a similarity between a stag's gracefully branching antlers and the delicate branching form of the yarrow plant.

*Camomile blossoms (*Matricaria chamomilla*) – Preparation 503*

This prep stabilizes nitrogen in the compost pile and also stimulates soil microlife, which aids plant growth. The flower blossoms are stuffed into the small intestine of a cow. The intestine is twisted into links like little sausages and buried in fertile soil over winter, ideally in a sunny spot where water from melted snow would fall. It is dug up around Easter.

*Stinging nettle (*Urtica dioica*) – Preparation 504*

Its purpose is to vitalize and enliven the soil. Nettles, cut when in flower, are buried in the soil for a year. Steiner believed that it would be possible to find local substitutes for all his suggested plant tonics except for the stinging nettle. Biodynamic growers in different parts of the world are looking for substitutes for the wild flowers that grow like weeds in Europe but aren't found in their locality. Having spent years in England trying to stop rampant nettle-beds from completely overwhelming my hedgerow, it seemed distinctly odd to see a neatly cultivated, freshly weeded bed of nettles growing on a biodynamic farm in subtropical Hawaii.

Oak bark (in Europe Quercus robur, *in the USA* Q. alba*) – Preparation 505*

This prep offers a strong healing force, helping to prevent disease. It is made from the bark of live oak trees, which is powdered and stuffed into the skull cavity of a domestic animal, preferably a cow, maybe a sheep or a goat. The skull is buried over winter in permanently moist ground, and dug up the following spring.

*Dandelion blossoms (*Taraxacum officinale*) – Preparation 506*

Dried dandelion flowers are stuffed into a cow's mesentery (the membrane that holds the intestines), and buried in the ground from autumn until the following spring.

*Valerian blossoms/garden heliotrope (*Valeriana officinalis*) – Preparation 507*

This prep is simply made from the juice of valerian flowers. It allows phosphorus to be utilized by the soil.

Natural pest and disease control

Oh, that sinking feeling: walking out into the garden early one summer morning and discovering the broad beans have virtually disappeared under a thick, sticky layer of blackfly or the cabbages have been completely massacred by caterpillars. The sight of pests strikes a chill into the heart of any gardener, and how they react to that sighting is what marks out a conventional gardener from an organic one and, in turn, an organic gardener from a biodynamic one.

For a conventional gardener, the solution is easy: turn to the ever-growing arsenal of poisons

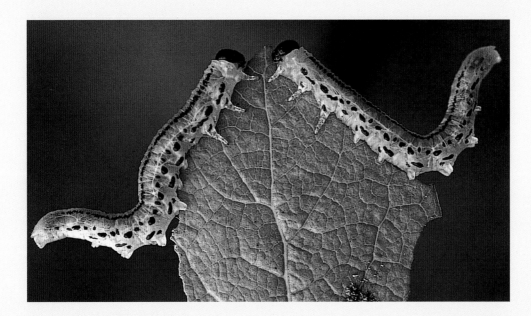

LEFT *Caterpillars in harmony with each other, though not necessarily the gardener. Rather than reaching for the spray gun when pests attack, ask first what might have caused the imbalance that allowed the pests to take hold, and what can be done to bring the garden into balance again.*

available, and spray the pests into submission. In doing so you may also kill off the pest's natural predators, making a recurrence of the attack more likely.

There are other problems associated with repeated chemical sprayings, too. The routine use of pesticides has been commonplace in agriculture for years, so one would assume that the percentage of crops lost to pests has decreased. The opposite is true. Pests have simply learned to adapt to the poisons and become resistant, so that the chemical companies have to produce increasingly potent potions in order to maintain the same kill rate.

The same is true with weeds: they too have become spray-resistant. This is something the makers of seeds genetically "modified" to resist weedkillers seem to overlook. They proclaim that the seeds are able to resist the weedkiller, so the crops will flourish while the weeds die. This, we are told, will lead to fewer sprayings; but the opposite appears to be true, and farmers are increasing rather than decreasing their use of weedkillers. Why? Two reasons. Firstly, because they know that using it will not kill off their genetically engineered crops, so they can spray with impunity to keep weeds down; secondly, more insidiously, because the weeds are developing resistance to those weedkillers.

Biodynamics looks at the big picture, realizing the interconnectedness of all things, while genetic engineering takes a very narrow view. Genetic engineering theory believes that altering genetic sequence A will have the single, totally predictable effect B, ignoring the fact that when unexpected elements interact with B they will produce reactions C, D, and E, possibly all the way to Z. Genetic engineering attempts to predict the unpredictable. The only thing that's predictable about it is that they won't produce the results expected.

The questioning approach

The organic gardener's approach to pests and disease is altogether kinder to the land, as it avoids synthetic chemicals in preference to mechanical barriers or companion planting to keep pests at bay and encourage beneficial insects. Some of these techniques are also useful to the biodynamic gardener (*see pp.101–2*).

The difference between organic and biodynamic approaches lies in one question. Before beginning to deal with a pest, the biodynamic gardener asks: *Why*? Why is this pest here? Why is it invading these plants and not others? Why are these weeds growing here? Why now?

There is a difference, too, between the mere presence of bugs and an overwhelming infestation. A biodynamic gardener acknowledges that there is room for a few pests in the garden and knows they do have their part to play. A biodynamic garden bursts with abundance, there is more than enough to go round, and a few leaves can be spared to the odd visiting caterpillar. Action needs to be taken when things get out of balance, and a crop threatens to become overrun. Problems must be carefully observed and the gardener ready to step in when things fall out of balance. Balance, once again, is the key.

What pests tell us

Pests show that there is something wrong with the soil. The theory is that healthy soil produces healthy plants, and healthy plants will not attract insects. For a plant to attract undue numbers of insects there must be something out of balance in the plant and, ultimately, in the soil.

Thus in the biodynamic method there are two prongs to dealing with insect attack, one dealing with the cause, the other with the symptoms. The first step is to discover what imbalance is attracting the pest in the first place, and taking remedial action to bring the land back into balance. Only then do we deal with the immediate symptoms. I like this approach because it means I can do something positive. It's not that all these terrible pests have somehow just fallen from the sky and infested the garden. If my garden is infested something is out of balance, and that means it's within my power to restore that balance.

In *Gardening for Health and Nutrition,* John and Helen Philbrick noted that two plants in a row of otherwise healthy broccoli were covered in aphids. They discovered that the infested plants had suffered root damage while transplanting. It was their weakened systems that had rendered them open to attack.

How can you create balance in the garden? First of all, by helping the plant grow on from seed to seedling to transplant as smoothly as possible. Plants that have been "shocked," for example by being planted out before they've been hardened off properly, will experience a setback to their growth. So, make sure things proceed smoothly. Hoe and water under the most helpful zodiac sign; don't scorch leaves or water with overly cold water on a hot day; use companion planting so that plants can support each other. Feed with compost and spray with liquid manure or compost tea. Regular steady feeding is better than overfeeding, which causes leggy growth that acts as a magnet to aphids.

Aphids

Aphids indicate over-rapid growth – indeed, the early spring growth of roses is so lush that aphids are just about unavoidable. A few can be rubbed off by hand, and a large infestation may be hosed off with water. Dealing with them on first sighting is generally enough to keep them in check, but it is a good idea to strengthen the plants using the method described below.

Fungal infestations

According to Steiner, fungus, mould, and mildew are the result of an imbalance of the moon forces – which influence water – in the soil. He believes that fungus lives in the soil, but when the moon forces become too active – a wet winter followed by a rainy spring, for example – those forces rise up in the plant, causing the fungal infestations that are so troublesome to those of us living in damp climates. The effects are most keenly felt when the moon exerts its concentrated energies on our planet, when the full moon (the time of greatest water activity in the plant and when sap is rising highest) coincides with perigee, when the moon is closest to the earth and thus its gravitational pull is strongest.

Horsetail tea – fungal prevention

The biodynamic remedy for fungal infestation features the common horsetail, *Equisetum arvense.* To make horsetail tea take some horsetail stalks you harvested in spring. Sprinkle 25g (1oz) of this dried herb in 570ml (1pt) of rainwater, simmer it for 20 minutes, and allow it to cool. This can then be further diluted before spraying, at a ratio of 570ml (1pt) decoction to 5.7l (10pt) rainwater, which should be enough to spray on 28sq m (300sq ft). This is the final biodynamic preparation, number 508.

Research by the Koliskos, two early pioneers of biodynamics, showed that this was particularly effective when potentized, that's to say diluted homeopathically. To potentize you need a supply of rainwater and two measuring jugs, plus a small lidded glass container for succussing (*see p.56*).

Take 27ml (1fl oz) of the original solution and add 250ml (9fl oz) of rainwater, then succuss it for two minutes. Then add 27ml (1fl oz) of this mixture to another 250ml (9fl oz) of rainwater, and succuss for another two minutes. Do this another three times, which will take it to a fifth potency, which the Koliskos recommend in their book *The Agriculture of Tomorrow*. Remember the more the solution is diluted the more potent it becomes.

The remedy above is actually a very forgiving one to make and there are several other effective methods. Here's another recipe: take a bunch of fresh horsetail tea and soak it in a bucket of rainwater for two weeks, until your nose knows of its presence. Strain it, dilute in about 36l (8gal) of rain or other pure water, and dynamize it as described for preparation 500 (*see p.58*), stirring to create alternating vortexes for 10 minutes, then spray on the land.

The best time of day to spray is morning, and I'd suggest spraying the whole garden with this in the spring. If the danger of fungal attack is high, such as in very wet years, spray three mornings running. An excellent time is just before a full moon-plus-perigee combination.

ABOVE *The ladybird or ladybug is a gardener's true friend. Not for nothing are they so celebrated in nursery rhymes and May Day festivities. Their role in aphid control is considerable, so it's worth encouraging beneficial insects such as these.*

Other uses:

• Good for strengthening plants against aphid attack, helping to prevent rampant, lush growth that acts as a calling card to sap-sucking aphids.

• Plants that can become watery, such as tomatoes and lettuce, will benefit from

several sprayings during their entire life cycle, starting in their pots or seedtrays.

• If the compost pile looks like it's getting waterlogged, spray 508 on it.

• Before transplanting vegetables into the cold frame spray the soil in it.

It really is one of the most versatile tools at your disposal.

Weeds

I know that weeds are just plants in the wrong place, but I tend to forget that when confronted by a thicket of couch grass or bindweed. What I'm really forgetting at that moment is that weeds have something to teach us, too. Thistles, for instance, point to compacted soil, while docks thrive in acid soil. Remedying the soil problem can cause those weeds to die back.

An obvious approach to dealing with weeds is repeated hoeing. Disturbing the soil to plant seeds has kicked the weeds into germination too, so hoeing can stop the problem before it starts. Hoe just before a full moon, when the seedlings' upward influences are at their strongest. Weed seed germination will be at its height at this stage in the lunar cycle, too, so your hoe will kill off weeds even before they've broken the surface. According to Thun the moon in Leo is also a propitious moment to hoe, as this is a time that also encourages seedling growth.

There are two ways to discourage weeds. The first is an infusion. Simply throw samples of the unwanted weeds into a bucket of rainwater and leave them until they rot, stirring occasionally on a leaf day. Then dilute, dynamize, and spray as for horsetail tea (*see p.85*). Don't expect a quick fix from this. It won't clear all the weeds overnight, or even in one season, but it will hold them back if you work at this over time.

Peppers

The second method is through fire rather than water, and again it's a long-term approach, known as "ashing" (because you burn the weeds to ashes) or

LEFT *A weed is only a plant in the wrong place. This picture of dandelions leads to the suspicion that they are just weeds to be eradicated, but in the previous chapter dandelions emerged as one of the heroes of the compost pile and a key remedy for healing the soil.*

"peppering" (because you shake the ashes on the land as if with a pepper-shaker). Gather the seeds of the weeds you want to eliminate. I know that one year's seeding means seven years' weeding and you need the seeds of the relevant weeds for this method. An alternative is to use the weeds' roots. When you have a nice parcel of seeds of various types, prepare to burn them. You need to do this over a wood fire, and the resulting ashes, wood, and other burnt material, so consider building a small wood fire in a barbecue tray. Wrap the seeds in a scrap of newspaper and put them in the wood fire. Be ready to partly cover the fire with a lid of some sort, because the seeds can spit and pop.

Let the seeds burn to a grey ash, and once they are cool, grind them in a pestle and mortar for an hour. The ground ash can be used in this form to disperse it – put it in a pepper shaker and scatter it. Better, though, is to potentize it – seven or eight times, by the method used for horsetail tea – and then spray it on the garden. Thun recommends doing the burning when the moon is in Leo, and spraying the garden with the liquid three times, each several hours apart.

Dealing with insects and other pests

This section is not for the squeamish. If you really can't stand slugs, look away now… The biodynamic way to deal with insect and other animal infestations is homeopathic – that is, treating like with like. This means that *eau de slug*, sprayed on the vegetable patch, will induce other slugs to stay away.

Again there are two options: fire and water. The water method needs 50 or so slugs, aphids, mosquitoes – whatever you want to work on – but with just one species at a time. Thun suggests doing this when the moon is in Cancer (a water sign, so the slugs should be particularly active). Place them in a bucket of water, close the lid, and leave them to macerate for a month or so; strain the liquid when the moon is back under Cancer again, and spray it on the affected areas. You'll probably need to repeat this cycle for several months – until you can't find enough slugs to make the new brew because your treatment has been so effective they've all been driven away.

An alternative is to ash the pests, by burning them on the barbecue, as before (*see p.87*). The various planting calendars offer extensive advice each month regarding the best times to do this work for different insects. The timings are quite exact, so it's worth checking carefully. Then either pepper the garden – put the ash in a pepper shaker and shake all over the garden – or dynamize a portion of the ash in rainwater and spray on the affected areas.

If you want to avoid having to do this, you'll need to create conditions that slugs don't like in the first instance. Use well-rotted mature compost on the garden, and give them no place to hide. If the garden has been mulched when dry and soon after there is heavy rain, you can be sure slugs will have taken up residence beneath the mulch, so it's worth considering removing it, or at least checking it thoroughly and repeatedly for infestation. You could also try spraying the Horn Quartz prep, 501 (*see pp.56–7*).

Incidentally, this method also works for other infestations, such as cat fleas – at least, if you can catch them, and if the cat will speak to you again after being sprayed with the resulting dynamized spray. You'll need to do it outside, or the fleas will hop off into the carpet, but spray the rest of the solution lightly over the carpets, just to be on the safe side. You could even give this method a go to keep termites at bay.

BELOW *Slug tea sounds unpleasant and it certainly doesn't smell very nice either. But, just as horses won't graze fields full of horse dung, so pests seem to be repelled by a spray made of that pest.*

Moles, voles, and mice

The ashing practice outlined for slugs also works for larger pests, such as moles. You need to burn the skin or pelt of the animal in question, and make a pepper or dynamized dilution from the resultant ash. This again needs to be timed very precisely to the zodiac – be advised by the planting calendar.

One important point: this is a localized approach. You need to gather from your garden the pests that are causing problems in your garden. If you are aiming to eradicate mosquitoes, for instance, then you need to try to obtain examples of all the different local species – there can be a surprising number, I've found. The pepper doesn't work as a generalized "mosquito" spray: it's specific only to those species you've collected. So if you decide to make a gerneral, all-purpose "anti-insect" spray, remember to collect examples of all the different kinds of aphids sucking at your crops. Output is only as effective as input.

There are some vertebrate attacks you just can't legislate for, however. Some years ago, in Kent – traditionally known as the "garden of England"– I had a delightful vegetable garden, separated from the sheep field next door by a 1m (3ft) high chicken wire fence. The first year, in my innocence, I planted a row of runner beans about 0.6m (2ft) away from the fence. They grew away splendidly, rapidly reaching the tops of the poles. One day, however, I came home to find they had been eaten; much of the stem had vanished from each plant, leaving only a small forlorn section or so at the top of the poles. Devastated, it took me a while to work out that the sheep must have reared up on their hind legs and propped their forelegs on the top of the fence in order to access my beans. Don't ever tell me that sheep are dumb.

ABOVE *The three steps to ashing are as follows: firstly, burn the pests on the barbecue, in an enclosed container such as an egg box; secondly, grind the resulting ash with a pestle and mortar; and, finally, dilute the mixture.*

Putting it into practice

Whether you're starting a garden from scratch or converting an existing garden from conventional practices to biodynamics, careful assessment of the strengths and weaknesses of your garden will give you a deeper understanding of your land and enable you to make the most of what you've got.

I think it's helpful to examine the land from the point of view of all four elements (earth, water, air, and fire/warmth), to gain a complete picture, and then marry this analytical, quantitative approach with your intuitive sense of what exactly your garden needs.

Even if the garden you inherit is in good shape, and you intend to continue cultivating it in pretty much the same layout, it's worth making the following observations and keeping notes. This practice really will help you begin to understand your patch of land better.

Earth

As a first step, draw up an accurate map of the plot: measure boundaries, notice contours. Is there a steep slope that will need soil-retaining plants or require terracing? Where are the permanent features, such as trees or water courses? Where is the best spot for the greenhouse or the compost heap? (Both need to have easy access to water.) Where will paths go? To decide this, watch where people walk for a few months and follow their lead, rather than deciding on a map and not looking at what happens in real life.

Examine our soil in detail. Is it chalky, clay, or sandy? How far down does the topsoil layer go? Do you have plenty of earthworm activity? Observe the effect of the passing seasons on the earth. Do you notice any frost hollows, low-lying land where pockets of frost may lie? You'll need to avoid planting frost-tender plants there. Notice which weeds favour your garden with their presence. Weeds can tell you a great deal about the condition and health of the soil (*see p.86*).

LEFT *It may take a while for your new garden to become as productive as the one shown here. While you're planning the layout, get started on making some barrel compost (see p.75) so that you can begin to enliven and heal your new plot as quickly as possible.*

LEFT *Water barrels don't have to be eyesores. Here, Clematis 'Miss Bateman,' trained across from a trellis, softens and brightens the water container.*

Water

Drainage is a key element in successful gardening. Does the soil drain easily, or does it become waterlogged? Does water accumulate in certain areas of the land and not others? If the soil drains water too easily, you can compensate for this by adding biodynamic compost, which will improve the soil's water-retention capacity; you may also do this by mulching, but find out how your soil performs before you can remedy any problems. Monitor the rainfall patterns. Obviously, monsoon conditions require a different response to rainfall than a temperate climate. Another useful thing to do is collect rainwater, both for general use and for dynamizing the biodynamic preps. Where can you site water barrels?

Air

Working with the wind is essential in any garden. From what direction does the prevailing wind blow? Is it dry or moisture-laden? In gardens near the coast or in the mountains, wind can take control by drying the ground, buffeting the plants, and blowing dust and dirt everywhere.

Victorians dealt with wind by building walls 3.6m (12ft) or more high, but with modern planning restrictions that's not an option available to most of us

Soil analysis

It's a very good idea to find out what happened to your garden before you came along. What was it used for – animal pasture, brownfield site, conventional chemical gardening? What inputs were used on the soil during that time? It's well worth having your soil tested for its chemical balance, humus content, and the possible presence of heavy metals. You need to be informed about any poisons left behind in your soil. Once you are aware of their presence you can do something about them. It'll be very rewarding in a few years' time to re-test the soil and see how much your biodynamic efforts have improved things. You should be rewarded by higher humus content, higher microbial activity, a decrease in persistent pesticides and heavy metal traces, and a more balanced ratio of the essential elements – nitrogen, phosphorous, and potassium.

It's worth getting a professional test done by a biochemical lab. A good test not only checks qualitatively for the elements present in your soil, it also tells you what elements are readily available for plant uptake, and analyzes the living qualities of your soil. Take the soil samples for analysis at the equinoxes rather than the solstices; microbial activity is much less intense at midsummer and midwinter.

today. In any case, wind is best not broken by walls but deflected by hedges, fences, or trees. A wall stops wind in its tracks, forcing it up over the wall and causing severe gusts and eddies on the other side, often wreaking havoc in the garden. Fences, on the other hand, let part of the wind through and attenuate its forces, diffusing the wind's energy.

A fence beneficially affects wind currents for a distance of several times its height. Build a fence or hedge at least 10 times as long as you expect its mature height to be, otherwise the wind will simply sneak around the sides of the fence and continue to cause problems in the garden. A particularly attractive option

LEFT *Two traditional windbreaks. On the far left is a towering brick wall from an old kitchen garden, complete with espalier-trained fruit trees. Though labour intensive, the fruit trees make great use of both space and warmth. The woven fence (near left) has clematis blooms poking through it.*

is the woven fence made from supple woods such as willow, ash, or hazel. This once-traditional craft form is gaining in popularity again. It makes a perfect backing colour for flowers and shrubs.

Fire/warmth

The path of the sun in relation to a garden is of crucial importance, especially where the growing season is short. What is your garden's aspect – does it receive morning sun, afternoon sun, next to no sun? If you plan to build a greenhouse, where is the sunniest spot? How much shade is cast by the house or outbuildings, or by overhanging trees, and where does that shade fall? Notice the range of maximum and minimum temperatures over the year; and take note of when the last frost of spring and the first frosts of autumn arrive.

There is a lot to be said for making the first year a time to get to know your garden, and also to build a compost pile or make Barrel Compost and spread it on the land, and then spray with 500 and 501. This way you're immediately getting started on the vital process of enlivening the soil, of waking it up to begin interacting with the elements and the available cosmic influences. It also gives you time to connect with all the entities engaged in helping you create your garden, if you choose to do so (*see Intuitive gardening, pp.120–7*). Tuning into your unique patch of land and understanding it properly before embarking on major changes and alterations is a great idea, but not one much in alignment with dynamic Western go-getting thinking. However, resisting the temptation to dive straight in and do something can pay rich dividends in the long term.

It's always a good idea to leave part of a garden uncultivated, where "weeds" and grasses can grow unchecked. This area will form a rich source of beneficial insects for the cultivated areas of the garden. Decide where the best place is for an uncultivated patch.

Paths

The benefit of grass paths is that they provide a habitat for many beneficial insects. However, in dry conditions they'll compete for water with the crops, and they also need regular mowing and occasional weeding – though, of course, if you keep mowing to flower days you'll need to mow less often. Paths made of reclaimed bricks look great. A downside is that they can be expensive,

but they do make an excellent choice in water-retentive gardens. Gravel will need firm boundaries if it's not to stray in among the vegetables and border plants. Woven path cloth can be bought by the metre and works well until it eventually splits, allowing weeds to poke through. No solution is ideal; it depends on your individual conditions and the materials at hand. The most ecological approach is to re-use materials you would otherwise throw out – even old carpet doesn't look too bad if it's turned hessian side up.

Tools

Buy the best you can afford, making sure they feel comfortable to use, and then look after them. You do get what you pay for, and since your tools are to last for many years, it makes sense to buy good quality. Handle tools in the shop and be especially particular when choosing a spade, making sure it's right for your height and not too heavy. I am fairly short, and there are spades designed for strapping lads that I can barely lift.

What tools do you need? Among the essential are a good spade for the heavy work of preparing the beds; a fork, for lifting potatoes; a hoe, for weeding; and a rake, for smoothing out the raised beds before sowing. A hoe is particularly important, because there is much hoeing to be done in biodynamics, not only for weeding (*see p.86*) but also to loosen the soil after rain, so that it retains moisture.

Hand tools, including a fork and a trowel, are also useful. A few baskets – the shallow trugs work well – a wheelbarrow, watering can, and…the list could go on and on. There's so much you can buy for the garden and so much that the garden centres want to sell you. I'd suggest starting small and gradually building up your collection of tools as you discover what you need for the way you want to work.

LEFT *A wonderful interplay of straight lines and curves, of flowers, vegetables, and ornamental vegetables, this garden delights all the senses.*

Garden layout

Do you want to grow vegetables and fruits in a separate area of the garden or include them in ornamental beds, integrating them into the overall shape? Where will you locate the vegetable garden? It is always handy to have herbs growing right outside the back door, so that they're almost within arm's reach. I prefer to have fruit and vegetables growing near the house, because I find that out of sight is out of mind. I want to be in as close touch as possible with my garden, so that I can notice any small changes as soon as they occur, and gently shift things back into balance before problems arise. My preferred vegetable garden layout is the formal potager (*see illustration on p.98*) because I find the shape aesthetically pleasing.

BELOW *Hanging your tools up in the same place every time means always being able to find them easily. It may also prompt you to maintain and clear them regularly.*

As a first-time gardener, start off with crops that are easy to grow and that do well in your soil and climate conditions. This may seem obvious but it is worth considering. Certain brassicas, for instance, or peas, are challenging for the beginner, while other crops, such as courgettes (zucchini) or french beans, grow wonderfully well and will reward you handsomely in your first season. Neighbours and local gardening clubs are rich sources of information on this subject. If you plan to start small in your first season, focus on salads and herbs. Both of these are often expensive to buy (it's also hard to find organically grown herbs) and will reward you with vastly improved freshness and flavour for relatively little effort. Runner beans are one of my all-time favourite crops to grow, sheep notwithstanding (*see p.89*), and I have grown tomatoes in pots on window ledges in lean times when I didn't have a garden.

Drawing up plans in the early stages will also help you monitor whether you have bitten off more than you can chew. It's important not to create more vegetable beds than you can comfortably manage. The garden should be a source of pleasure, not a tyrant demanding more attention than you can spare.

The vegetable bed

There are many systems for arranging vegetable beds, but I'm going to focus on the one I prefer: raised, double-dug beds. This is a method much favoured by biodynamic gardeners. Raised beds curve gently towards the centre, with a difference in height from the edge of between 5cm (2in) and 25cm (10in); I'd say that a differential of 10cm (4in) or 12cm (5in) is ideal. The raising improves drainage and lifts the plants gently towards the sun, enabling them better to take advantage of the cosmic forces bouncing around them. Plus, the older I get, the more I appreciate not having to bend down quite so far.

Double digging is, of course, extremely hard work in the first year; but after you've put in that initial backbreaking work, you can avoid any further digging in future. You improve the soil structure this way, because beds that are never walked on are never compacted. This loosened soil has vastly improved drainage, and plants will be able to put down roots with far less effort, resulting in bigger, sturdier plants. It also has much better aeration, improving plants' ability to breathe. All you have to do in subsequent years is add small quantities of biodynamic compost, which will increase the humus content and replace

LEFT *A formal potager such as this is a way of having lots of easily tended beds for flexible crop rotations and spaces for perennial vegetables and fruit.*

nutrients absorbed by the previous crops. Detailed instructions on the use of compost are given in the chapter on biodynamic composting (*see pp.66–79*).

Preparing the vegetable bed

This is the hardest work of all, but take heart, as it only has to be done once. Digging to a depth of 0.6m (2ft) loosens the soil and allows plant roots to penetrate with far less effort than in compacted soils. This means the plants can be spaced more closely than in a conventional bed, which increases the shade cover each plant gives to the soil and thus reduces the amount of water the plants need; it also reduces the number of weeds that can grow (provided that the bed is well weeded until the plants are big enough to give this cover). That's why the width is so important – never make a bed wider than can be reached from both sides. A width of 1.2m (4ft) is a good guideline to follow, but people with a long reach could manage a wider bed if desired.

Double digging

This is the practice of digging down through two spade depths of soil. The most crucial thing to remember with double digging is the importance of keeping the topsoil separate from the subsoil. The top 15cm (6in) of soil is the richest in nutrients, humus, and earthworms. Subsoil is just that; living below the surface, it supports the topsoil but does not contain the same level of nutrients. Burying topsoil beneath subsoil means that many of the beneficial bacteria and microorganisms, most of which reside in the top 7.5cm (3in) of layer one, will be killed off, and it will take years to get the soil back into good condition. Make sure that the topsoil stays where it belongs. This applies regardless of how much topsoil you have, in terms of soil strata.

In the following instructions I refer to the top spit of soil as layer one and the lower spit as layer two. This is to avoid confusion with the actual topsoil and subsoil, because topsoil layers in gardens can run from 15cm (6in) to several metres (feet) in depth. It is important to choose the moment for this task with care. If the soil is too dry, it will be impossible to push the spade in, and if it is too wet, digging will damage the soil structure.

1. When the soil is just damp, weed it, then lay a board at least 0.6m (2ft) wide across the bed. From here, dig a 30 x 30cm (12 x 12in) trench along the width of the bed. Put the layer-one soil you dig out into a wheelbarrow and remove it.

You may need it to fill in the end of the bed, but as this process aerates and loosens the soil, so that it increases in volume, you may find it's not needed. If this is the case it will be perfect for the small layers of soil you need when building the compost pile. Dig as even and as level a trench as possible, using a flat-edged spade. Loosen all the soil to the same depth.

2. Next, take a fork, get in the trench, and dig down into the second layer. Do not remove this earth, but loosen it as thoroughly as possible to a depth of 30cm (12in). Push the fork in as far as it will go, then work the tines backwards and forwards for maximum aeration.

3. Now move the board back and dig a second trench next to the first one, shovelling the layer-one soil into the gap left by the removal of the earth in the first trench. When shovelling, try not to turn the layer-one soil; keep the top of the spit uppermost when placing it in the empty trench.

4. Loosen the layer-two part of the second trench with a fork, as before. Stop soil from the adjoining layer sliding into the newly created trench; keep layer one and layer two soils as separate as possible. When the entire bed has been dug over, add in the layer one soil removed from the first trench if it is needed to fill it.

The bed should not need double digging again unless something happens to compact it. Be sure not to tread on the bed, as that will undo all the good you have just done. To reach the centre of the bed, stand on the digging board to spread your weight.

OPPOSITE *These plant combinations may look pleasing, but companion planting could have brought better flavour and improved disease resistance. While onions and cabbage are mutually beneficial, parsley offers more benefits to tomatoes or asparagus. The lettuce on the left would be better off helping the strawberries pictured on the right, while the chives would have been more beneficial planted with carrots.*

BELOW *Double digging. From left to right: 1. Dig as even and level a trench as possible with a spade. 2. Fork through the subsoil then dig a second trench alongside the first. 3. Fill the first trench with the topsoil from the second trench.*

You don't have to double dig, of course. Like anything in gardening, there's a counter-argument for whatever anyone suggests. So-called "no-diggers" point out that there's no digging in nature, which is of course true; but any form of gardening is an unnatural practice, the result of human will imposed on nature, which means that we have to compensate for what we do, and that includes adding compost and working the soil. A second rule is to dig once and not again, because too much digging can certainly be detrimental to soil structure.

Companion planting

This is a system of planting for mutual support. Certain plants, when planted next to each other, ward off each other's bugs. Some help others to thrive in their presence. The opposite is also true, and there are plants that don't do so well next to others. Fennel, for example, is antagonistic to virtually every plant. Mutual antagonisms are to be avoided, and positive friendships encouraged. Companion planting helps the garden grow into a richly varied ecosystem, and it is worth nurturing as wide a variety of plants as possible. Interplanting, where several different plants are grown close together, encourages plants to share their beneficial, symbiotic influences. This effect is amplified in the many small beds of garden layouts such as the potager.

A classic example of companion planting is the "Three Sisters" used by Native Americans, who interplant corn, beans, and squash. The climbing beans use the corn stalks as support, the low-growing squash offers ground cover which suffocates weeds, and the beans provide nitrogen.

The key to companion planting, from a biodynamic point of view, is to have all four aspects of the plant represented: root, leaf, flower, and fruit. This encourages maximum balance and harmony in the garden. You can usefully balance deep- and shallow-rooting plants, as well as tall- and shorter-growing ones. Positioning quick-maturing crops next to slower-maturing ones, also known as catch-cropping, maximizes the available space. A quick-growing crop, such as radishes or lettuce, is harvested before a slower-growing one – cabbage, for example, needs the space.

Herbs have a multiple function: besides their healing properties and their flavours, they help ward off pests. Sage, rosemary, and thyme keep away the cabbage butterfly. Aphids are repelled by nasturtium, spearmint, nettles, or garlic.

Green manures

There are two schools of thought about what should be done with overwintering vegetable beds: leave the soil bare or plant it with a cover crop. I believe that we should follow nature here. Nature, as we have seen, will immediately work to cover any earth laid bare. If we follow her lead we will be preventing soil erosion and growing crops that can be dug in, to feed the soil. Green manures, such as field beans or winter tares, also help earthworm activity by acting as insulators, keeping the earth warmer in winter and cooler in summer. One important thing with green manures is always to dig them in just before or around the time they flower. Leaving it later means that nitrogen content decreases, and if they seed you'll be dealing with them for decades.

Crop rotations

This can be seen as companion planting over time: a sequence of planting that benefits both soil and plants. Crop rotation helps to avoid the build-up of pests in the soil, and also balances out the depletion of nutrients and minerals. The four-field system of crop rotation introduced in Britain during the 18th century immediately helped to improve soil fertility. Particularly important in this scheme was lying fallow; the putting out of use of each field one year in four to allow it to rest and recover from the unnatural practices of agriculture. In terms of demands made on the soil there are three groups of plants:

- Heavy feeders, which make great demands on the nutrients the soil contains, include plants such as cabbage, lettuce, leeks, and tomatoes.
- Soil improvers, the legumes (peas and beans), which fix nitrogen in the soil.
- Light feeders, mostly root crops, such as carrots, onions, and beetroot.

A traditional crop rotation would proceed as follows: start by spreading compost on the vegetable bed, then plant heavy feeders; follow this with a legume, which restores some of the nitrogen taken by the heavy feeders; then add a light dressing of compost and plant the light feeders; decide whether to add a fourth element to the rotation with a green manure such as buckwheat; or simply start the cycle again with compost and heavy feeders.

A biodynamic approach recognizes the influence of the four elements expressed in plant growth. This involves separating out into different parts of the rotation the root, leaf, flower, and fruit/seed crops. Start with the leaf crops, which are mainly heavy feeders; follow this with flowers, which, as it were, tread lightly on the soil; next grow fruit/seed crops, which are most of the legumes; and finish with root crops, which covers the majority of the light feeders.

In practice, there aren't any commonly grown vegetables that fall into the flower category, so many people leave flowers out of the rotation equation; however, that needn't be the case. I love having extra flowers for cutting, but I don't like to cut from my flower garden because it spoils the display; it's

ABOVE *Broccoli, part of the cabbage family, is a heavy feeder. Most people grow it just for the flowerets, but the leaves are also edible, particularly when young and tender.*

LEFT *Strawberries get their name from their origins as meadow or grassland plants, growing in the remains of dead grasses. Mimic this cultivation by providing them with a thick mulch of clean straw.*

therefore worth my while to grow extra flowers in the vegetable rotation, where I can cut away to my heart's content without it troubling me aesthetically. This is also the place to grow helichrysum and other flowers for drying. An alternative to flowers is to plant potatoes in that part of the rotation.

Strawberries that receive the biodynamic preps and equisetum spray can be kept in the same bed for four years, so plan to integrate new strawberry beds into the rotation every fifth year. Strawberries should follow your root vegetables, and be replaced by leaf vegetables.

Crop rotation is both an art and a science. The art lies in creating a sequence of crops that reflects the needs of each plant, of the soil, and of your kitchen, because you don't want to be forced into growing quantities of something your household doesn't care to eat simply to fill up the rotation.

Seeds and seed saving

Everything starts with the seed – so much depends on it. Where will your seeds come from? Purchased seed has been produced in another part of the country, or even in a different country altogether, and what thrived there won't necessarily be too happy in the conditions prevailing where you live. Often seeds are bred for commercial needs, such as uniformity of size and regular maturing, the opposite of what the home gardener wants. They are unlikely to have been biodynamically produced and probably not organically-produced, either, and it will be impossible to tell what chemical treatment they may have undergone.

If you need to buy seed, check first for biodynamic suppliers (there are a few) or organic seedsmen. Biodynamic seed is, of course, ideal, because of the extra vitality such seeds will contain, but organic is infinitely preferable to chemical-based seeds because organic seeds will not have been weakened by pesticides and fungicides. A good source of seeds could be your local biodynamic gardening group, especially if a seed-saving initiative has been set up. Seed savers can select those plants that have performed most productively in their particular growing conditions. Not only do savers produce seeds that have already benefitted from the biodynamic preparations and optimum cultivation times, but they are acclimatized to local growing conditions. One of the original impulses for biodynamics lay in the desire to improve seed fertility, so it seems imperative for biodynamic gardeners to preserve the life-forces that they have so carefully instilled into their plants by saving seed rather than buying it. Imagine what kind of life-force is – or is not – present in a seed that has been genetically altered by terminator technology to make it sterile. What does that do for the life-force of the food that seed will produce?

Seed saving also contributes to the preservation of old seed varieties. Many seeds are becoming unobtainable because of regulations that support big seed growers at the expense of small gardeners. Some seed varieties have

BELOW *Preserving the garden's harvest is an essential part of the annual gardening cycle and it is important to choose the right moment for harvesting. Pick flowers for drying on flower days (left) and harvest root vegetables on root days (right).*

even become extinct. Seed saving can contribute to restoring biodiversity in the garden. Never save seeds from hybrid varieties, however – in fact it is preferable to avoid them altogether. They look showy but they are hard to grow and won't breed true, i.e. what you see this year is not what you'll get next year.

Watering

Use the daily rhythms to help you. Water the soil rather than the plants, so that leaves won't get scorched on hot days. Heat and wind will both speed up water loss in plants so that the need for water in these conditions may be greater. Use the calendar, too, and concentrate your watering efforts at times when the moon's influence is strongest.

Crops and the four elements

Throughout this book the different effects each of the four elements has on the plant world in the form of improved garden results have been explored. Working with the elements in planting, weeding, and harvesting can increase yield, aroma, and keeping quality.

Root – earth

These are plants harvested for their roots: beetroot, carrot, celeriac, garlic, onion, parsnip, potato, radish, salsify, shallot, swede, and turnip. Plant, cultivate, and harvest all these vegetables on root days. Although the potato is a tuber rather than a root, it still falls into this category. Potatoes like a good feed of biodynamic compost in the planting trench.

While planting at moon apogee tends to cause vegetables to bolt, potatoes like to be planted then; you can plant also them at new moon because roots and tubers are less affected by the watery upward part of the growth cycle than other plant groups.

Young beetroot tops are a sadly neglected part of a leafy root vegetable. Don't put them on the compost heap but steam them as an alternative to spinach.

Leaf – water

These plants are harvested for their leaves, and are associated with the water element because leaves tend to be the most watery part of the plant. Here are some examples: asparagus, cabbage, cauliflower, kohl rabi, lettuce, spinach, and Swiss chard. Cauliflower could be classified as a flower, but the plant is harvested when the flower heads are immature and it responds to leaf treatment best. Broccoli, on the other hand, much prefers flower days.

Maria Thun recommends harvesting leaf vegetables (especially cabbage) on flower days if they are for storing rather than immediate eating. She also suggests that chicory should be planted on leaf days but subsequently cultivated on root days to ensure strong roots, then harvested, and replanted on leaf days again. Mowing the lawn on leaf days will encourage fast growth, while working it on flower days will slow its growth, useful information if you want to cut down on time spent behind the lawn-mower. Thun's book *Gardening for Life* contains exhaustive detail on planting and harvesting times for most vegetables and fruits, should you want to pursue this avenue of research in greater detail.

Flower – air

All flowers, including those grown to be dried, for medicinal use, and for cutting, benefit from planting, cultivating, and harvesting on flower days. Flowers also keep for longer when cut on flower days. It's a shame florists don't work by the planting calendar!

Fruit – fire/warmth

Not only does this category include obvious fruit including pears and apples, but also any plant where the fruit or seed is eaten, such as beans, courgette (zucchini), cucumber, grapes, and peas. If you like to make jams or jellies, or

bottle or freeze your fruit, Thun recommends this work is carried out on a fire/warmth day.

Other rhythms to work with

You can also follow the principle that leaf qualities are emphasized by the waxing moon while root qualities are heightened by the waning moon. This mirrors the daily rhythm, where picking in the morning is best for lettuce and picking in the evening is best for beetroot.

Successional sowing

Successional sowing, or sowing small amounts of seed at 10- or 14-day intervals, is the best approach for home consumption as opposed to market gardening. Sowing in this way ensures a steady supply of each crop through a maximum-length growing season.

The biodynamic planting calendar makes this particularly easy. Using the calendar, there are only one or two occasions each month when the auspices are good for sowing a particular kind of crop. I sit down with the calendar during my planning phase, before the beginning of the gardening season, and plan ahead. I make specific notes on the calendar, which I find much easier to follow later in the season than trying to work out in my head when I last planted lettuce or beans, for instance.

The biodynamic gardening year

I've arranged this season by season, rather than month by month because the length of your growing season is different to mine and is different again to someone who lives elsewhere. Weather conditions vary from year to year, as well. This means that you need to temper any advice telling you what to do when – whether from this section or a planting calendar – with your own awareness as a gardener, and your assessment of the prevailing conditions in your garden.

Winter

An unusual place to start, in most gardening methods, because this season is generally believed to be the time when the garden lies dormant, waiting for the spring sun to warm it and start it into life again. But, as we have seen, this is not so in biodynamics. On the contrary, life-force is strongest in the

RIGHT *In these highly expressive Arcimboldo prints depicting the seasons of the year, winter shows little but bare roots (right), emphasizing the activity beneath the earth that takes place to support the rest of the cycle. Then spring (far right) bursts into bloom.*

earth during the winter. The sun's rays angle deep into the soil, and there is little surface growth or activity to prevent its entry.

Winter is, of course, the time to plan ahead – to review the results of the previous season, to work out next season's rotations, and to order seeds. But it is also the period to get to know your garden in a new way. When the weather permits, spend time out there, just tuning in to the apparent quiet and becoming aware of the vibrant activity going on beneath the surface of the soil. Gardening jobs include pruning, lifting any remaining root crops, and turning in any winter cover crops.

Spring

For me, this is the most exciting time in the gardening year, as it is when the growing season begins. Spray 500 (*see pp.56–7*) one evening just before dusk, to enliven the soil. In early spring, sow hardy brassicas, broad (fava) beans, lettuce, onions, and spinach. In mid-spring, depending on local conditions, direct sow your hardy root crops, and start tender seeds such as tomatoes in your greenhouse or on a windowsill in a sunny aspect.

Stick to your planting plan and remember your successional sowings. In late spring, begin hardening-off the frost-tender plants, and plant them out in cloches or a cold frame when the weather permits. Spraying 501 will help the hardening-off process.

Summer

As we move towards the solstice, the upward growth spurt intensifies. Once the danger of frost is past, plant out frost-tender vegetables such as beans and re-pot any tomatoes. If the latter are to be grown outdoors, now is the time to transplant them.

Use the calendar to your advantage. Wait until after the summer solstice before planting out biennials; that way you'll take advantage of the beginning of the downward phase, the contraction. Planting before the solstice, while the garden is still in its upward phase, is likely to encourage bolting.

It's also vital to keep weeding, weeding, weeding. Keep an eye on the watering, and be prepared to mulch if the soil gets very dry. If it rains while a mulch is down, remove it or make regular checks underneath it for slugs (*see pp.87–8 for control*). Harvest courgettes (zucchini) and beans regularly, or they will stop fruiting.

In late summer, as space becomes available, plant out autumn and winter crops. Now is the time to think ahead to saving seed and to choose which plants will go to seed. Begin harvesting and drying the herbs you have grown for winter use.

Without doubt this is the busiest time of year for the gardener, when all your careful planning should pay off. It is also when you will begin to see the results of your labours with the compost pile and the spraying of the preps.

ABOVE *Summer shows the results of the root activity of winter and the flowering of spring, bringing forth its harvest (left) Autumn, depicted in more mellow colours, shows the final harvest of long-maturing fruits such as grapes (right).*

Autumn

This is the fruiting season, the time when the contracting, downward, gravity forces really start to become apparent. Sow winter spinach and corn salad (lamb's lettuce) in early autumn, and plant out garlic cloves. This is a time of much work in the kitchen, when fruit and vegetables are preserved for the winter. Most years my grandmother needed to make a vat of green tomato chutney to deal with her tomatoes that didn't ripen, and chutney really is a wonderful way of putting otherwise-unusable produce, be it underripe or the results of a glut, to good use. String up the onions, put the vegetables in store, make jam, and blanch and freeze beans. Incidentally, many books say you can't freeze strawberries successfully, but my mother used to purée her surplus crop before freezing, which worked very well.

Clear the garden of debris and build the compost pile – it's good to get it started before the frosts come. As autumn progresses past the equinox, mulch overwintering crops with straw.

Seed soaking

Another way of using the preps is as a seed soak. The moment of germination is said to be one of the most propitious times to introduce the influence of the various preps, and what better way to do this than to actually moisten the seeds with the preps just before germination?

Prepare a unit of 500 (*see p.56*) by stirring for an hour, then stir the seeds around in the liquid. Plant the seeds immediately. Some gardeners suggest that the seed responds so well – with improved germination and higher productivity per plant – that less seed is needed. Monitor the results and decide for yourself if these claims are true.

Biodynamics in the kitchen

You don't need me to tell you just how bad food matters have become – people are writing about it everywhere you look. New facts come to light every week about the dreadful state of our diet, and how our health and immune systems are threatened on all sides. Repeated studies have shown that fruit and vegetables contain decreasing levels of essential minerals, vitamins, and trace elements. Many of the fats that we consume are hydrogenated, which denatures once-healthy polyunsaturated fats. As Sally Fallon points out, hydrogenated vegetable oils are implicated in cancer, diabetes, and obesity.

Many domestic animals are now treated abominably, intensively farmed, and routinely fed supplements of antibiotics. At the time of writing, in the USA cattle are even fed genetically engineered growth hormones to force faster, more profitable growth. Commercially raised turkeys require artificial insemination, because the males crush the hens if they try to mate. Astonishingly, some animals are even losing their natural instincts, no longer knowing how to graze. Eric Schlosser charts the appalling degeneration in the food we eat, the way it is produced, and the damage done by those who produce it, in his book *Fast Food Nation*.

In 1924 Rudolf Steiner predicted that feeding meat products to ruminants would send them mad. BSE has vindicated that prediction. Rachel Carson rang a warning bell in 1962 with her book *Silent Spring*, which led to the establishment of the Environmental Protection Agency, but it seems that despite these warnings the destruction of habitats and poisoning of air, water, and earth continue little checked.

Modern food production is light years away from the practices of the late 19th century, and the majority of the most dramatic changes have happened since the 1960s. The building of motorways and freeways and the development of cheaper air freight have led to food being hauled across countries or even continents for our consumption. Locally produced food is rarely available in supermarkets, which is one of the reasons for the recent resurgence in farmers' markets – that way, shoppers can meet the people who produce the food they're buying and can find out exactly where it came from and what was done to it. I go out of my way to buy biodynamically produced flour for bread-making, and I only wish it was more widely available.

The rise in food allergies, heart disease, other degenerative diseases, asthma, and attention deficit disorder is all linked to diet. The presence of pesticides such as dioxin in the food chain; the wasteful over-use of plastic packaging, some of which transfers to the food; the secretive

LEFT *Buying certified organic chickens, or purchasing them from a biodynamic farm, ensures you are supporting more humane farming practices. These chickens are not fed antibiotics, steroids, animal by-products or hormones, and are guaranteed outdoors access – a far cry from the life of a battery hen.*

LEFT *Bake your own bread using organic or biodynamic flours, or support local bakers who follow traditional methods.*

introduction of untested, unproven genetically engineered foods; and the huge amount of hidden, low-grade fat and white sugar in processed food are all partly to blame for this rise. Never was "you are what you eat" a greater truism than today; Western populations are overweight, sickly, and lethargic, with compromized immune systems.

Steiner recognized the link between degenerating diet and increasing apathy as long ago as 1924, when he said, in *Agriculture*: "Nutrition as it is today does not supply the strength necessary for manifesting the spirit in physical life. A bridge can no longer be built from will to action. Food plants no longer contain the forces people need for this."

What Steiner intended was for biodynamics to revitalize the waning life-force in plants, to strengthen us as humans to build that bridge from will to action: to not just think about doing something but to actually go out and do it. The planet is in trouble, and we need the will to take action to mend things. It's not too far-fetched to imagine that biodynamic food can supply that willpower. It has been proved in repeated studies that biodynamically grown food contains more vitamins, minerals, and trace elements than either chemically- or organically grown food. (*See* Science Magazine, *May 31 2002, p.1694.*)

Food in season

Although we've become divorced from seasonal rhythms, with many foods available all year round, eating food in season does keep us in touch with the deep-seated natural rhythms that are still a part of us. It's the same instinct that makes us yearn for rich stews and casseroles full of root vegetables in winter or light salads in summer. These seasonal rhythms change us with the seasons, typically making us more withdrawn and introspective in winter, and more lively and outgoing in summer. The fruit and vegetables that surround us at these different times of year are there for a reason – they support our different states of being. It can help us make the inner adjustments to the change of the seasons if we make conscious choices to eat the food each season brings.

Use the minimum amount of heat or water to cook the food. Having gone to all that effort to raise the vital forces in the food, it's important to preserve them as far as possible. Any cooking will destroy some of the life-force in food.

Soups have so many advantages it is difficult to know where to begin. They're cheap, nourishing, and filling, and a perfect way of using up leftovers and outer leaves or stalks. I sometimes peel woody broccoli stems and throw them into soup, for example. For the soup stock I use water leftover from boiling or steaming vegetables. And since I acquired a hand blender, the mess of ladling portions into the liquidizer is gone forever. It's also heartening to note that several weight-loss experts suggest starting a meal with soup, saying that it aids metabolism. Steiner himself advocated beginning every meal with a vegetable soup, noting that its warmth helps the digestive process. The biodynamic garden offers rich resources for making that soup varied and interesting.

LEFT *Imagine if this picnic were created from local eggs and cheeses, homebaked bread, and fruit and vegetables from your own garden . . . food in season, produced locally. Nothing better for flavour, and light on the earth's resources, and not a morsel air-freighted in from another country.*

Cooking with the four elements

It's interesting to see how the elements of earth, water, air, and fire/warmth make their presence felt in various cooking processes. For more information on this, see Mier and Hoogewerff's book *Fundamentals of Nutrition in the Light of Spiritual Science*.

Fire/warmth

Of the four this is the most obvious element in the cooking process, the one first used and harnessed by early man. Fire can be seen as the furthest reach of the sun's ripening process, finishing a series of actions begun by the warmth and heat of the sun, taking root and leaf vegetables through to the final stage of the four-fold development, fruiting. Fire can also be added to food through the use of spices.

Water

This element is an equally obvious cooking mechanism, but it must be used with care. Overboiling leads to decay and the loss of nutrients, including water-soluble vitamins. Steaming is a better method than boiling for lightly cooking, as it retains flavour and nutrients. Keep the leftover boiling or steaming water to use in soups or stocks. The water element also materializes during cooking – spinach, for example, contains so much water that it can cook in its own juices.

Air

Air is the baker's friend, the alchemy of bread and cakes, whether induced by eggs, baking powder, self-raising flour, or yeast. The physical act of whipping and beating add air and volume to a meringue.

Earth

This element appears in cooking, too. Many baked or grilled foods cook to a crisp crust; rice pudding, for example, forms a firm skin. Even a meringue has a crisp outer layer. These foods offer us something to chew on, a sense of eating something that is part of a definite whole.

The ideal approach to menu planning involves including vegetables and fruit from each of the four elements, where possible. This could mean balancing root vegetables such as potatoes with leafy green salads and fruits including tomatoes, then throwing some flowers, such as nasturtiums, into the salad bowl. Edible flowers always look so inviting in a salad, and they add the harmonizing influence of that element to the meal. When I was packing the weekly boxes for a community-supported agriculture scheme, we always used to make up little posies of flowers for each box. It seemed important to round out the food package to all four elements, and even though the flowers weren't necessarily edible, I knew people receiving the boxes really appreciated it.

What to cook on

The choice of what kind of stove to use isn't necessarily one you'd associated with biodynamics, but some interesting studies were carried out by Dr Rudolf Hauschka, a student of Steiner and founder of a toiletries and cosmetics house. He boiled distilled water on stoves of gas, electricity, wood and straw, then used the cooled, boiled water as a growing medium for wheat plants. The results indicated the different heating media enhanced growth to different degrees. He noted that the water heated by electricity had the least effect on the growth of the wheat plant, followed by gas, then coal, then wood, with straw having the most favourable outcome on the growth of the seedlings.

This doesn't surprise me. When I was in France researching wine books, the best part of the day was a stroll at dusk through the village where I was staying, breathing in the piquant aroma of wood-smoke as the locals came home from work and lit wood fires for the evening. There is probably also something that reaches back into our primitive hunter-gatherer ancestry about cooking on an open flame, which is why so many men enjoy barbecuing.

Dr Hauschka conducted his experiments in the 1950s, before the advent of the microwave oven. I suspect that a repeat experiment in the 21st century would put microwaves firmly at the bottom of the list. Microwaves heat liquid in a way unlike any of the conventional methods above, all of which transmit a form of radiant heat. The author Sally Fallon (*see p.139*) notes that microwaves were put on the market without much evidence about what happens to our bodies when we eat food that has been microwaved, and that as a result we are all unwitting participants in a worldwide experiment. She points to studies showing that they cause changes in vitamin content and availability, and may also have unfavourable reactions on fats and proteins.

LEFT *Take vegetables fresh from the garden and slice and skewer them before placing onto a waiting grill – here, you have lunch in minutes, tasting even better cooked over hot coals in the open air.*

What to cook in

Hauschka also examined the effects on water of the vessel it was heated in. He boiled some distilled water in gold, earthenware, porcelain, enamel, glass, copper, tin, iron, and aluminium pots, again germinating wheat seeds in the cooled water. His best results came from the gold pot, reinforcing all those fairy tales about eating off gold plates. He even found that stirring water with a gilded spoon had a similar effect. The sequence of results is as given in the list on page 118, with aluminium being the least effective – and this study was made long before the scares implicating aluminium in Alzheimer's disease.

The secret additive: TLC

There's no getting around it: food tastes better if the cook's having a good day. Have you ever noticed the difference between the food you make when you're rushed, running late, tired, angry, upset – you name it – and the meal put together when you feel calm, relaxed, content, as if all's well with the world? Somehow the food prepared and cooked when you're in a good mood tastes better than when you're not. Just as in intuitive gardening, our intentions colour what we do and how well we do it.

It certainly aids digestion as well as enjoyment to be in a calm, relaxed, state of mind when eating, not least because it means that the food will be chewed for longer. This is the vital first step in digestion, one that is all too often cut short by people eating in a rush. Tender loving care (TLC) for both cook and diners, that's what's required. And biodynamically grown raw materials, of course.

Intuitive gardening

When we walk into a room and feel the tension hanging in the air, when we say "you could have cut the atmosphere with a knife," what do we mean? What are we perceiving? Certainly nothing that can be seen, heard, touched, tasted, or smelled. It's a feeling, a sense of "something in the air." This thing that you are just aware of, without necessarily being able to give a sensory-based explanation or logically argued reason, is your intuition at work. Science hasn't been very tolerant of intuition since scientists decided that the mind and body were separate, and that the only permissable knowledge was that gained through the five senses. Modern scientific method accordingly demands objectivity. This separation of self as "scientist" from the object of one's study is a recent development in human thought. The ancient Egyptian king and alchemist Hermes declared in *The Emerald Tablet*: "what is above is like what is below, and what is below is like what is above." In other words, we're all part of the same whole.

Nature does seem to bear this statement out. If you start to look, you'll notice that Hermes was right, and that the microcosm does indeed resemble the macrocosm. The spiral of galaxies echoes the spiral that forms in a vortex of water, whether it's the one visible when a bath is emptied or the one created when a prep is stirred. Wolf Storl in *Culture and Horticulture* offers repeated proofs of these parallels. One of these is the dance of the planets – the patterns that they make in their orbits around the sun aren't circular but interwoven. Those very patterns are found in nature, such as in an apple. Slice through the core of an apple to see the same pattern as the planetary path of Venus.

Unfortunately, these kinds of similarities and parallels tend not to cut much ice with modern scientists. Goethe's approach to scientific work was remarkable for its attempts at synthesis, using both science's rigorous observation and the intuitive awareness demanded of practitioners of the arts. This is what is currently referred to as using both the intuitive right brain and the rational left brain, or, if you will, the harmonizing of conscious and unconscious thought processes.

Goethe used this approach in his study of plants. He reasoned that in order to appreciate fully a plant in all its many-levelled glory he needed to open up his inner being to enable himself to perceive more than his five senses could offer him, to expand awareness. He called this developing new "organs of perception". Rudolf Steiner took this notion further, and expanded it into a way of thinking he called "supersensible perception". This way of perceiving therefore allows the use of our five senses and other senses, such as sense of well-being and sense of balance (both literal and metaphorical). This approach was anathema to followers of Isaac Newton, and a clinically detached form of observation was the only acceptable scientific approach until quantum physics forced scientists to realize that another form of perception was necessary. When they studied the movement of sub-atomic particles, they discovered that the act of watching changed that which was observed. Did the particles therefore have consciousness? Does this prove that it is impossible to observe "objectively"?

Intuition is another way of describing things that aren't verifiable by the five senses, but that somehow we still know to be true. Women are held to be more intuitive than men, but that may simply be a result of upbringing. Some boys are still encouraged to button up their feelings and think logically, whereas it's acceptable for girls to express the intuitive side of themselves more freely. Happily, both men and women today are working to balance the two sides of their nature. You can even find classes devoted to developing your intuition.

What does intuition mean in the garden? Two things, I think, both of which are related. First of all, it's a part of the need for close observation of the soil, the plants, the weather, the continual subtle shifts in day and seasonal and moon rhythms, and learning from that direct experience. Some people have become so attuned to the different "feel" of their garden under the many planetary aspects that they can tell without looking at a planting calendar when the moon has shifted into a different planetary constellation. That's not an innate skill but something that can be learned through years of observation and self-training. All of us gardeners, if we focus on it, can learn to develop our own perceptions and awareness.

LEFT *In Arthur Rackham's world, a parallel universe of fairies and elves toils in the garden. What if a raft of nature intelligences were just waiting to offer their assistance in the garden? How much more productive would your garden be if you could tap into that source?*

Secondly, intuition means the chance, if we wish to take it, of harnessing yet another force to aid us in creating the best possible fruit and vegetables: calling on the help of the nature intelligences.

Findhorn

Probably the connection most people make when they hear about gardening with nature spirits is to Findhorn. This is a community founded in 1962 by Peter and Eileen Caddy and Dorothy Maclean. The beginning was not promising – a caravan site on a wild part of the northern Scottish coast, with sand for soil and no funds to improve it. They established contact with entities connected with each different plant they grew, called devas. The devas, or spirits of the plant kingdom, they learned, had a role in fostering the development of each plant and they had very definite ideas about how humans should interact with them. They also made contact with what they called elementals: the spirits of earth, water, air, and fire/warmth. Their guidance was straightforward and pragmatic, ranging from how far apart plants should be spaced and how much water they needed, to advice on thinning versus transplanting lettuce seedlings (thinning was preferred).

The proof of the effectiveness of their approach grew there for all to see. Within three months the gardens brought forth the most astonishing fruits and vegetables, of a size and quality not seen before in these harsh local conditions. The garden became an oasis of vitality and fertility amid virtually desert conditions, producing 18kg (40lb) cabbages and broccoli stems that were almost too heavy to lift. Today, the Findhorn Community has grown to several hundred members and welcomes over ten thousand visitors a year, offering courses in biodynamics and many other ecologically conscious practices.

Guidance on water

I began reading about nature spirits when I went to work on a biodynamic farm in Hawai'i. Three weeks after I arrived, the farmer left for an extended visit to the east coast of the USA, and I felt nervous about the resulting responsibility after so little time there. One morning at sunrise I sat down in a shady spot at the centre of the garden to see if there were any nature spirits around, and if so, could they please help me to make sure that I didn't mess anything up in his absence? To my amazement, no sooner did I focus my question than I heard an insistent little voice say: "stop watering us so much!"

RIGHT *Every garden needs a wild area, somewhere for wildflowers to self-seed, and beneficial insects to find sanctuary. It is not the size that matters, but your intention to leave a spot uncultivated, turned over to nature. You can enjoy it too as a perfect place for contemplation.*

I was completely taken aback. The farm lay in an arid valley with next-to-no rainfall. The farmer had left a rigid watering schedule for me to attend to. Surely the crops would need all that water? Apparently not. Surreptitiously, I cut back on the amount of water I had been instructed to give to the plants. I did not kill anything off in the farmer's absence – on the contrary, the plants thrived. I realized I had tapped into a source of mutually helpful dialogue, and was beginning to learn to trust my intuition.

Using intuition in the garden

I think it's important to treat your plants with respect. Some people believe in giving their plants 24 hours' notice that they are to be transplanted or potted on. This can result, they suggest, in the plant's cooperation. Whether or not you warn the lettuce seedlings that they're to be planted out the next day, acknowledgment is important. Plants are, after all, living entities, so it's good not to treat them as inanimate objects.

Dr Christiane Northrup, in her health guide, *Women's Bodies, Women's Wisdom*, notes that performing repetitive, rhythmical physical movement is a great way to allow your intuition to come forward and speak. She points out that repetitive movement increases the brain's alpha waves, the state that fosters intuition. Double digging or the gentle rhythm of hoeing offer perfect rhythmical exercises that fit into this model.

How to expand awareness

There are many different ways to develop the use of your intuition. A useful first step is to get into the habit of using peripheral vision when you're in the garden. The normal way of seeing is called foveal vision, also known as "tunnel vision," where only what lies directly ahead is seen. Foveal vision is used when we're concentrating on the task in hand.

Peripheral vision, on the other hand, involves expanding your awareness to take in everything around you, focusing on the far reaches of your visual field. This can be practiced by sitting and concentrating on a spot in the distance of the garden, slightly higher than your sitting height. Then, while focusing on it, allow your awareness to move to the far corners of the garden. This will create a relaxed yet alert state of mind, one used by many, both for meditation and for excellent performance in sports or martial arts.

Try this out one afternoon while working in the garden. Just expand your awareness using peripheral vision, then hold on to that awareness while carrying out your normal tasks. You may find that the awareness allows you to connect with the garden in quite a different way. Steiner also devised a series of mental exercises, known as the six basic or subsidiary exercises, designed to train people to be observant without judgment and preconception, offering gardeners the perfect way to "see" in the garden. It's up to you how far you take these ideas. Of course I can't prove that there are fairies at the bottom of the garden, but on the other hand I can't prove that they are not there either.

Perelandra – working with nature intelligences

If you're interested in pursuing the idea of working with nature intelligences, what many people call "co-creating" the garden, I recommend two books by Machaelle Small Wright, *The Perelandra Garden Workbooks I* and *II*. The author gives practical instructions on how to go about contacting nature intelligences and how to put that work into practice.

LEFT *A perfect harvest of Cox's Orange Pippins, picked on a fruit day and collected in a trug, a traditional harvesting basket.*

Biodynamics and the future

If biodynamics is such a good thing, why hasn't it swept the planet? I think that there are two reasons why it has been slow to catch on up until now. First of all, it requires a little time and effort to get to grips with the principles involved, to understand what needs to be done in the garden in order to make biodynamics work for you. It certainly doesn't offer the "quick fix" of a box of synthetic fertilizer. It takes time, which is something that we generally think we're so short of.

Secondly, there's not much of an opportunity to make megabucks through supplying gardeners and farmers with biodynamic products. Even with organic gardening, there's money to be made in selling "organic" pest-control sprays and fertilizers and potting compost. But the real money is made in chemical agriculture, where the big biotechnology companies lock farmers into repeat purchase of their products, year after year. "Terminator technology", where seeds are genetically programmed to die at the end of the season so that farmers cannot save seed for re-use the following year, is an obscenity in countries such as India where farmers have saved seed for centuries. Imagine what would happen if biodynamic methods swept the planet. Can you imagine Monsanto operatives burying thousands of cow horns?

The economic advantage of biodynamics is that it allows you to become almost totally self-sufficient in the garden. The purchase of fertilizers and fungicides, including organically approved ones, will not be necessary. Apart from equipment such as wheelbarrows and forks, all that's needed are the preparations, and these can be made in tandem with a local biodynamics group or even, eventually, by yourself. With practice and patience, you can also save seeds. This is one of the reasons why biodynamics is gaining popularity with farmers in developing countries such as India, a powerful alternative to the economic and cultural enslavement that follows when farmers sign up for genetically engineered seed.

Flowforms to cleanse water

Taking the theme of self-sufficiency further, the cleaning-up of contaminated water by the use of flowforms (*see pp.62–3*) is an unexpected side benefit of using these contraptions. To paraphrase British designer, socialist, and poet William Morris (1834–96), I don't just believe flowforms to be beautiful; now I know them to be useful.

The rhythmical pulsing of the flowform is perfect for dynamizing the preps, but its potential applications range far wider than that. Many experiments have been conducted in the use of flowforms for purifying water, based on the fact that swirling water through a flowform in repeated, rhythmical figure-of-eight patterns has the effect of oxygenating it. This power of oxygenation means that flowforms have great potential as a means of purifying grey water – it's not too far-fetched to imagine that the self-sufficient suburban household could one day take charge of re-using most of its own water wastes this way.

And, even more of a challenge, the wastes produced by dairy or pig farms, which cause such headaches for neighbours enduring the smell and water treatment authorities overwhelmed by the amount of slurry they have to deal with, can be treated and transformed by flowform use.

In his book *Grasp the Nettle*, Peter Proctor describes putting cow dung slurry into a flowform, adding the compost preps, and setting it going. After running the flowform for about six hours, he reports, the liquid had almost completely lost its pungent smell.

Radiation

It's possible that biodynamics can go further than this, and have a healing effect on the deadly poisons mankind produces. In *Biodynamics* magazine, Fall 1989, Maria Thun observed that after the nuclear-weapons testing in 1958 there were significant levels of strontium-90, a radioactive isotope, in plants. Some of us will recall that there was a significant scare at the time about strontium and other heavy metals turning up in cows' milk, and thus entering the human end of the food chain. Thun noticed that plants growing on limestone contained significantly lower levels of this poison, so she set out to test the effects of giving different forms of lime to plants. She experimented with materials such as oak bark (which is already part of Steiner's plant medicine chest), limestone itself, basalt, snail shells, and eggshells, and discovered that no strontium was found in plants when she applied basalt and eggshells. Next Thun looked into how best to introduce these materials to the plants, and found the most effective method was to mix basalt and ground eggshells into cow manure. This was the origin of Barrel Compost (*see pp.75–6*). According to Thun, this preparation has also been used to beneficial effect in Russia on farms affected by Chernobyl radiation.

Because Barrel Compost, contains all the biodynamic compost preparations, it is the best way of getting the healing effects of the preps on to your land

BELOW *The gifts brought by the three biblical kings to the infant Jesus: gold, frankincense, and myrrh. Today, some people in biodynamics are using these substances to help heal the earth.*

quickly, rather than waiting a season for a compost pile to ripen. This is the ideal way to approach a new garden: build your compost pile for next season, and make Barrel Compost for this one.

The three kings

Another contribution to the healing work of biodynamics was made by Hugo Erbe (1885–1965), a German biodynamic farmer. The impetus for his work described below dates back to 1945, to the fal-lout from the allied bombing of Hiroshima and Nagasaki.

Recognizing their beneficial influence, Erbe had built up an extremely strong connection to the nature spirits on his farm, but in the wake of the nuclear bombings he noticed a huge disruptive influence around the farm: a mass flight of the elemental beings from his land. Anxious to bring the elementals back into balance and back to his farm, and to heal the deep damage done to the earth by the dropping of these bombs, he turned to the Epiphany story in The Bible and developed a healing preparation made from the gifts brought by the three wise men to the infant Jesus.

As any carol singer knows, the gifts bestowed by the Magi were gold, myrhh, and frankincense. Gold signifies the riches of the material world. It comes from deep inside the earth, and symbolizes durability – hence it's what wedding rings are usually made from. It is also the gift of tribute paid to a king. And gold survives fire.

Frankincense is very fragrant when burned, and in biblical times it was used during religious observance as a devotional offering to the gods. Myrrh is bitter, and was used to embalm the dead; it also had pain-numbing qualities, and was included in a drink offered to Jesus just before his crucifixion. Myrrh represents human suffering and the triumph of life over death.

Erbe blended these three together on the night of December 31, as the old year passed into the new, a time alive to special possibilities. Then he waited until the Twelve Days of Christmas were over – Twelfth Night is January 5 – and on January 6, Epiphany or Three Kings Day, he dissolved the powder in some warm rainwater and dynamized it for an hour, just as for Horn Manure (*see pp.57–9*), holding his intention to connect with his nature spirits all the while. Then, just as for Horn Manure, he sprayed it along the boundary of his farm and throughout the property. Kits for making Three Kings Preparation can

be bought from the biodynamic associations, which stress that it should only be used on gardens that regularly receive all the biodynamic preparations (500–508).

How do you quantify the results of such a spraying? This is impossible with current scientific measuring devices, of course. You'd have to be in contact with the nature spirits in your garden in the first place in order to know how they respond to such an offering, and that's not necessarily a topic that is easily discussed.

Biodynamics is a science that is not readily measured and quantified by conventional academic scientific tools; as mentioned earlier, science turned away from this world-view before Goethe's time, and a materialistic, mechanistic view has dominated ever since. But that doesn't mean it's the only view, or the right one. Just because we can't (yet) measure something, it doesn't mean that it doesn't exist. Biodynamics has the power to facilitate enormous worldwide healing, but only if we act as agents for that healing, by observing, communicating, stirring, sowing, weeding . . .

Some people in biodynamics say that you can't properly understand the workings of biodynamics unless you are an anthroposophist, that you need an intimate understanding of Steiner's spiritual theories in order to make the practical work of biodynamics really effective. This is not true, in my opinion. I have seen grape growers practice biodynamics on a purely pragmatic level, and get improved results.

I have also seen that those who follow the methods of biodynamics find themselves gradually drawn into a greater spiritual understanding of the forces at work – the unseen, invisible things that can't yet be measured by science. Slowly, biodynamics becomes part of a process of spiritual development. That was true for me, certainly. The more I do the daily, seasonal, annual practical work in the garden, the more I observe the tiny changes happening around

LEFT *Demeter, Greek goddess of the harvest, was the figure chosen by biodynamic farmers in the late 1920s to represent their produce. Today, Demeter certification, used by fully tested and accredited biodynamic producers, covers a wide range of foods.*

me all the time, and the deeper my understanding and awareness becomes. It is not necessary to embark on a process of spiritual growth in order to "do" biodynamics; but you may find it happening all the same, as you tune into the powers of nature and to the cosmos beyond.

I believe that gardening has the power to heal on a much wider scale than one's own patch of land. Tending the earth, healing the damage that has been done, allows us to tap into deeper rhythms, to connect with each other and with the planet itself. There is so much that needs to change if the planet is to recover, and it is heartening to see that so many campaigns and coalitions are forming to fight against genetic modification, the poisoning of the earth and the water, and inhumane treatment of food animals.

Growing our own food seems like a simple thing to do by comparison – so simple that it often passes campaigners by. It doesn't make headlines or stir the heart like pictures of birds dying after an oil spill. But just imagine what life would be like if we all produced at least some of our own food, and did so biodynamically. It would mean the end of groundwater poisoning with pesticides and no more experiments with genetically engineered crops. Wildlife and biodiversity would return to the land.

As I hope I've shown in this book, biodynamically grown food simply bursts with vitality and life-force. The difference between eating a biodynamic apple and an irradiated, chemically sprayed apple could, over the long term, even mean the difference between life and death. Biodynamic food can give us the willpower to develop both physically and spiritually, giving us more strength to fight for the preservation of the planet.

ABOVE *Some of the finest wines in the world are made from biodynamically grown grapes, and more and more top producers are converting their vineyards to biodynamic methods, because they know that this way of working brings first-class results.*

e oint octombre est dit le nombre de .vii. qui senifie u
le ql estoyt dit roy des charles doz/car en son temps

aumcnr.

calirc.

oran.

hr applique & catutitis:
un dinott uiltemcnt:·

Resources directory

Rudolf Steiner's philosophy and methods are not just found in biodynamics – he wrote and lectured prodigiously and influenced many other areas of life. His collected works, books plus transcribed lectures, run to over 350 volumes. He spoke about painting, sculpture, architecture, medicine, cosmology, bee-keeping, and spiritual science. He devised a means of making speech visible, of expressing sounds through physical movement, called Eurythmy. His work in education has been particularly significant.

EDUCATION – THE WALDORF SCHOOLS

In the 1920s Steiner was invited to help establish a school for the children of workers at the Waldorf-Astoria cigarette factory, in Stuttgart, Germany. That's why these "Steiner Schools" are often known as Waldorf schools. Steiner created a holistic system of education that fosters all aspects of a child's growth: the physical body, its vital life-forces, its emotional identity, and spiritual well-being. Rather than making the school a "machine for learning", the Waldorf curriculum reflects and supports the child in all aspects of its development. Waldorf schools now flourish all over the world, and are probably the most visible sign of Steiner's legacy.

WELEDA, DR HAUSCHKA, ANTHROPOSOPHICALLY EXTENDED MEDICINE

Weleda was the name Steiner gave to the products a group of scientists and doctors began to produce in Switzerland in the 1920s. Today Weleda produces a range of homoeopathic and anthroposophical remedies, plus toiletries and skin care, available all over the world. These plant-based remedies are mostly grown biodynamically.

The approach taken by anthroposophical medicine goes beyond that of conventional medicine, just as biodynamics goes beyond conventional gardening. Conventional medicine sees the body as a machine, and if the machine breaks down it is medicine's job to repair the fault. Steiner's view was that a human is composed of a mind and a spirit as well as a body, and that all three need to be taken into consideration when treating a patient.

An early student of Steiner's, Dr Rudolf Hauschka, studied the making of plant-based remedies and experimented extensively with Steiner's methods. Today, the company he founded in 1921, WALA, makes over 5,000 anthroposophic and homeopathic remedies and over 100 Dr Hauschka Skin Care holistic preparations, which are available in 30 countries. The company tends award-winning biodynamic gardens and also runs the business itself according to a socially responsible model advocated by Steiner.

CAMPHILL COMMUNITIES, KARL KÖNIG

These are supportive therapeutic communities where adults with learning disabilities live and work with adult helpers, none of whom receives a salary. Founded in Britain in the dark days of 1940 by Austrian refugee Karl König, who based his concept on Steiner's writings, the communities have spread across Europe and the USA. Each community has a different emphasis, but many run biodynamic farms, where everyone can find a role suited to his or her ability, and contribute positively to the well-being of the community.

COMMUNITY-SUPPORTED AGRICULTURE

For those who can only garden in window boxes there's still a way to connect with biodynamic farm life: through Community Supported Agriculture. This movement began with biodynamics and has spread to include many organic farms as well. A farm, or market garden, sells "shares" to a group of willing local supporters, often city dwellers or those unable to garden. The cost of the shares is designed to cover all the farm expenses, and in return members of the supporting community all receive a box of produce each week throughout the growing season. Supporters both benefit from bumper crops and share the loss in the event of failure, such as a hailstorm hitting the ripening strawberries. Supporters frequently become deeply connected with "their" farm, volunteering at harvest and participating in other ways. Others do no more than receive their weekly box, yet are happy in the knowledge that they are supporting local employment and eating the best possible food. Contact your local biodynamic association for lists of nearby biodynamic CSA schemes.

FURTHER READING

I make no apology for including books that are not available everywhere, or even that are out of print. Thanks to internet searches and online shopping I have bought books from halfway around the world and found the most obscure out-of-print books lurking in online secondhand bookshops.

Biodynamics

Steiner, Rudolf. *Spiritual Foundations for the Renewal of Agriculture*, (translated by Malcolm Gardner), Bio-Dynamic Farming and Gardening Association, Inc., 1993. The source of inspiration for all the information in this book. A challenging read, requiring much prior knowledge.

Storl, Wolf. *Culture and Horticulture, a Philosophy of Gardening*, Bio-Dynamic Literature, 1979. A stimulating, eclectic read, one of my favourite books on biodynamics.

Robison, Dave. *Introduction to Biodynamics*, http://www.oregonbd.org/class/class-menu.htm. This excellent introduction is freely available online. It draws on many sources and is particularly interesting for its scientific proofs.

Thun, Maria. *Gardening for Life: The Biodynamic Way*, Hawthorn Press, 1999. A fount of detailed information on working with Thun's planting calendar.

Kolisko, E. and L: *The Agriculture of Tomorrow*, Kolisko Archive Publications, 1978. This book is long out of date: I obtained a copy through my public library, although a re-issue has been talked about for some time.

As discussed in the chapter What is Biodynamics?, this book is intended as a guide to what's specific about biodynamics. It is not meant as an exhaustive guide to those aspects of gardening shared by organics and biodynamics. For more information on organic-gardening techniques, any book by Geoff Hamilton will provide excellent practical guidelines, should you wish to flesh out the information

mentioned here. Another good practical guide is by John Jeavons. *How to Grow More Vegetables* (6th edn, Ten Speed Press, 2002) derived some of its philosophy from Steiner's work, and is an excellent practical gardening guide.

Nutrition

Fallon, Sally: *Nourishing Traditions*, 2nd ed. New Trends Publishing, Washington D.C., 1999. This is a fascinating debunking of the many myths about modern nutrition, and encourages us to avoid hydrogenated fats and processed food; it includes a mass of eminently sensible and practical advice, and a collection of several hundred putting-it-into-practice recipes. Highly recommended.

The disasters of modern agriculture

Kimbrell, Andrew (ed.). *Fatal Harvest: The Tragedy of Industrial Agriculture*, Island Press, 2002. Over 40 well-researched essays detailing the devastating effects on our health, the economy, and the environment of industrial, chemical-based farming.

Schlosser, Eric. *Fast Food Nation, the Dark Side of the all-American meal*, Perennial, 2001. A relentless indictment of the way we eat now, with terrifying implications for health and sanity.

Water

Schwenk, Theodor. *Sensitive Chaos*, Anthroposophic Press, 1990. The inspiration for the flowform lies in these pages. This book teaches you to understand the meaning and movement of water. After reading it I doubt you'll ever look at a river in the same way again.

Genetic engineering

Anderson, Luke. *Genetic Engineering, Food, and our Environment*, Green Books, 1999. This book is an excellent British-based survey.

Cummins, Ronnie and Lilliston. *Genetically Engineered Food: A self-defense guide for consumers*, Marlowe & Co, 2000. Another excellent book, this time written from an American perspective.

Working with the moon

Paungger, Johanna and Poppe, Thomas. *The Art of Timing*, Saffron Walden, 1996. A really useful account of all aspects of working with the moon, right down to the best time of the month to do the washing or scrub mould off the shower tiles. Fallon, Sally. *Nourishing Traditions*, 2nd edn, New Trends Publishing, Washington D.C., 1999. A fascinating book that debunks many myths about modern nutrition, and encourages us to avoid hydrogenated fats and processed foods – a mass of eminently sensible, practical advice and a collection of several hundred recipes, which out that advice into practice.

USEFUL WEBSITES

USDA research on the effects of biodynamic compost preps can be found at http://www.nal.usda.gove/ttic/tektran/data/000009/06/0000090623.html

HELPFUL ORGANIZATIONS AND ADDRESSES

Biodynamic associations:
UK: http://www.anth.org.uk/biodynamic
North America: http://www.biodynamics.com
Australia: http://www.biodynamics.net.au
New Zealand: http://www.biodynamic.org.nz
These organizations will be able to assist you with buying

the biodynamic preparations detailed in this book, and help with sourcing planting calendars.

DEMETER

Demeter, the Greek goddess of the harvest, gives her name to the international trademark by which biodynamic produce can be identified. It's not just fruit and vegetables, but also meat, flour, bread, cheese, jam, Darjeeling tea, and even woolly underwear.

WINE

I came to the study of biodynamics through meeting winemakers passionately involved with it and I still believe that

RIGHT *Every garden needs a wild area, somewhere for wildflowers to self-seed and beneficial insects to find sanctuary. It is not the size that matters, but your intention to leave a spot uncultivated, turned over to nature. You can enjoy it too, as it makes a perfect place for contemplation.*

there's nothing like biodynamic agriculture to bring out the clearest, most vibrant expression of the land and its produce. I also don't think it's coincidence that some of the world's greatest winemakers grow their grapes biodynamically. These are, after all, people who care passionately about quality. So if you're looking for excellent wines to complement your exquisite biodynamically produced food, look out for these producers, or check the website of wine merchant T&W Wines (www.tw-wines.com) who devote part of their wine list to biodynamics; many of their selections are internationally available.

SOME BIODYNAMIC WINEMAKERS

New Zealand: The Millton Vineyard.

France: Ostertag, Zind-Humbrecht (Alsace), Huet, Didier Daguenau, Clos de la Coulée de Serrant (Loire), Guy Bossard (Muscadet), Guillemot-Michel, and Leroy (Burgundy), Chapoutier (Rhone), Pelisson, and Fouques (south of France).

Steiner believed that alcohol, although once helpful for human development, is no longer necessar for us. (I don't think it's necessary, either, but I do think that good wine with good food is a great pleasure.) The practical effect of this is that the Demeter associations in some countries do not certify biodynamic wine. This doesn't mean to say that wines from these countries aren't made from biodynamically-grown grapes, simply that they can't obtain certification to say so.

Steiner once said that there were two types of people engaged in his work: the older ones, who understood everything but did nothing with it, and the younger ones, who understood only partially or not at all, but who immediately put his suggestions into practice. There is an art to combining these two opposites. There is, of course, far more to know about biodynamics than this book can cover. You can spend a lifetime – many already have – developing an ever-deepening understanding. But the only way to really learn about biodynamics is to get out there and do it. It doesn't matter how you get started, really, the point is to take that first step. And I wish you much joy in accomplishment, and delight in discovery, on your way.

Index

Page references in italics refer
to illustrations

A

agriculture 7–8, 12–15, 16, 17, 22, 36
aphids 25, 84, 85, 89, 102
ashing 86–7, 88, 89
autumn 29, 31, 35, 61, 111

B

beetroot 48, 103, 106, 108
broccoli 103, 107

C

Caddy, Peter and Eileen 124
calcium 25
camomile 78, 79
Camphill Communities 18, 131, 138
carbon 25, 44
carrots 31, 44, 48, 103, 106
caterpillars 82
cauliflower 107
chemicals
    in biodynamics 25, 44, 56, 79
    fertilizers 9, 14–15, 16, 17, 22, 25, 67–8
    in food 9, 113–15, 131
    pest control 16, 54, 81–2, 114, 130, 135
    for weeds 82
chicory 48, 107
circadian rhythms see rhythms of nature
Community Supported Agriculture 137
companion planting 8, 24, 83, 84, 101–2
composting
    barrel compost 74, 75–7, 92, 132–3
    bins 70
    with herbal remedies 55, 62, 68, 71–2,
        73–6, 79, 86, 132–3
    ingredients 68–9, 70, 132
    siting 69–70
    starters 74
    uses 73, 93, 98–9
container growing 14, 107
cooking 116–19
cows 64, 65 see also manure
crop rotation 102–4

D

dandelions 79, 87
Darwin, Charles 35
Demeter certification 134, 138, 141
Descartes, René 15
development of biodynamics 8–11, 18–21,
    129–35
double-digging 98–101, 126
Dr Bach flower essences 54
drainage 93, 98

E

elements 41–2, 43
    in composting 72–3
    in cooking 117–18
    in garden planning 91–2, 93
    in pest control 86, 88
    and plants 42–3, 44, 48, 106–8
equinoxes 31–2, 111
Erbe, Hugo 133

F

Fallon, Sally 113, 118, 139, 140
fences 94–5
fertilizers
    chemical 9, 14–15, 16, 17, 22, 25, 67–8
    natural 9, 12, 13, 14, 25, 54–65, 130
    see also composting
Findhorn Community 124
fleas 88
flower clocks 30, 33
flowers 30, 43, 46, 48, 103–4, 105, 107,
    117–18
flowforms 62, 63, 130–1
food
    biodynamic 10–11, 111, 115–19,
        135, 137
    modern production 9, 14, 17, 113–15
    organic 7–8, 114
    seasonal 28, 115–16
frankincense 133
frost 33, 34, 35, 61, 92
fruit 47, 48, 103, 107–8, 127
fungal infestations 25, 39, 53, 55,
    84–5

G

genetic engineering 82–3, 114, 115, 135
Goethe, Johann Wolfgang von 16, 18, 122
gold 118, 119, 133

H

Hahnemann, Samuel 56
harvesting 30–1, 34, 35, 127
Hauschka, Dr Rudolf 118–19, 138
health issues 9, 22, 23, 106, 113, 114–15
hedges 94
heliocentricity in plants 32
herbal remedies
    in composting 55, 62, 68, 71–2,
        73–5, 76, 79
    dynamizing 57–9, 63, 72, 85, 133
    making 55, 57–9, 63–4, 84–5, 130
    storing 64–5
    using 59–62, 85–6, 111
    see also individual preparations
herbs 34, 48, 97, 100, 102, 110
Hippocrates 41, 56
hoeing 84, 86, 96, 126
holism 9, 16, 24, 54, 55
homeopathy 53, 56, 85
horn preps see preparation 500;
    preparation 501
horsetail tea 84–6
hydrogen 25

I

insects, beneficial 24, 83, 85, 95
intuitive gardening 51, 121–7

K

Keats, Brian 49, 51
Kolisko, Dr Lilly 19, 39, 85, 139
Kolisko, Eugen 19, 85, 139
Konig, Karl 138

L

ladybirds 85
leafy vegetables 30–1, 45, 48, 103, 106,
    107, 108, 109

legumes 14, 25, 39, 47, 48, 103
Liebig, Justus von 14–15
Linnaeus, Carl 33

M

Maclean, Dorothy 124
manure
    animal 13, 14, 23, 45, 56, 63, 71, 74–7
    green 14, 21, 102, 103
moles 88
moon
in biodynamics 9, 25, 38–9, 46, 48, 84, 108
influences 34–5
lunar cycles 36–8, *39*, 48, 108
lunar nodes 38, 48
in pest control 84, 86, 87
mosquitoes 89
mowing 95, 107
Müller, Paul 16
myrrh 133

N

nettles *78*, 79
Newton, Isaac 15–16, *17*
nitrogen 15, 16, 25, 44, 56, 79, 103
Northrup, Dr Christiane 126

O

oak bark 79, 132
organic gardening 8, 21, 22, 67–8, 81, 83, 130
oxygen 25, 44

P

paths 92, 95–6
pest control
    chemical 16, 54, 81–2, 114, 130, 135
    natural 8, 25, 55, 83–6, 87–9, 101, 102, 130
Pfeiffer, Ehrenfried 19, 74
Philbrick, John and Helen 83–4
phosphorus 25, 79
planetary influences *see* moon; sun; zodiac
planning a garden 91–6, 97
planting 10, 11, 34, 39, 51, 84
planting calendars 38, 48–51, 108
potagers 97, *98*
potassium (potash) 25, 79

potatoes 39, 48, 106
preparation 500 56, 59, 60–3, 64, 71, 109, 111
preparation 501 56–7, 59, 61–3, 64, 65, 88, 109
preparation 502 71, 79
preparation 503 71, 79
preparation 504 71, 79
preparation 505 71, 79
preparation 506 71, 79
preparation 507 72, 76, 79
preparation 508 84–6
Proctor, Peter 39

R

radiation 131–2
rain 72, 93, 110
rhythms of nature
    annual rhythm 29–30, 31–2, 33, *34*–5
    daily rhythm 30–1, 43, 45, 106, 108
    expansion/contraction 28–30, 37, 110
    monthly rhythm 34–8
see also seasons
root vegetables 31, 44, 48, 103, *105*, 106, 108, 109

S

salad crops 30–1, 45, 48, 85–6
Schwenk, Theodor 44, 48, 139
seasons 28, 29–30, 31–2, 33, *34*–5, 61, 108–11, 115–16
Sedgman, Philip 130
seeds
saving 104–6, 110, 130
soaking 111
sowing 38, 39, 108
silica 25, 56
slugs 87–8, 110
soil
    analysis 92, 94
    fertility 9, 12, 13–15, 17, 68, 102
    healing 9, 11, 19–20, 21, 54–5, 68
    imbalances 54, 83, 84
solstices 31, 32, 37, 110
spring 29, 31, *34*, 61, 109
Steiner, Rudolf
    biodynamic principles 9, 18–19, 22, 25, 39, 42–3, 54, 138
    healing practices 11, 106

    on healing soil 9, 19–20, 54, 59, 78
    herbal remedies 54, 78, 79
    on nutrition 115, 116
    on perception 122
    on pest control 84
    philosophy 9, 17–18, 134, 138–9
Storl, Wolf 122, 139
strawberries 28, 100, 104, 111
sulphur 79
summer 29, 31, 32, *34*, 37, 110
sun 9, 31–2, 33, 37, 42, 43, 44, 45, 95

T

termites 88
Three Kings preparation 133–4
Thun, Maria 45–6, 48–9, 75, 86, 87, 107, 131–2, 139
tomatoes *8*, 48, 97, 103, *106*, 109, 110, 111
tools 96, *97*, 130
Tull, Jethro 14

V

valerian 72, 76, 78, 79
vineyards *24*, 134 *see also* wine

W

Waldorf schools 18, 42, 138
walls *12–13*, 93–4
water barrels 93
watering 84, 106, 110, 124, 126
weeds 30, 82, 86–7, 92, 110
Weleda 136–7
Wildfeuer, Sherry 49
wind 13, 93, 94–5
wine 21, 135, 141
winter 30, 31, 33, *35*, 37, 61, 108–9
worms 68, 69, 73, 77, 92
Wright, Machaelle Small 127

Y

yarrow 79

Z

zodiac
in biodynamics 37, 42–51
in pest control 86, 87, 88, 89
plant groups 44–8

Author's Acknowledgments

Joan Simmons and Reginald Case, my mother and her father, who showed me how to love a garden.

Nicolas Joly, who first inspired me to study biodynamics, and Michel Chapoutier, who lent me my first copy of Agriculture. These two passionately committed winemakers and biodynamists first opened the door.

Everyone who so kindly read various drafts and gave such thoughtful feedback: Fr. Philip Harmon, Helen Kimball, Twyla Mitchell, Jerry Altwies, Dave Robison, Anthony Nelson-Smith, Cheryl Kemp, Rosslyn Dawson.

My long-suffering agent, Anne Dewe, and Rachel McKenna: sorry about last time.

Dennis Carroll, for opening new doors. Eileen Bristol and Louise Frazier, for help with nutrition. Graham, for absolutely everything.

And to all the staff of Kahumana Community: Fr. Phil, Chris, Helen, Annie, Dick, Robert, Uli, Christian, Lucas, Jon, Lance, Bob, Mohsen, Sooriya, Sai, Johdi, Ganga, Diana; and to residents past and present. The idea for this book took root in your gardens. Mahalo nui loa for nurturing it, and me.

Picture Acknowledgments

Mitchell Beazley would like to acknowledge and thank the following for their permission to use the photographs in this book.

Key: a above, b below, l left, r right, OPG Octopus Publishing Group

1 John Glover; 2-3 OPG/Stephen Robson; 4 Derek St Romaine; 6 Andrea Jones/Garden Exposures Photo Library; 8 Clive Nichols/Clive Nichols Garden Pictures; 10-11, 12-13, 14 Andrea Jones/Garden Exposures Photo Library; 15 Bridgeman Art Library/Collecton of the Earl of Leicester, Holkham Hall, Norfolk; 17 Bridgeman Art Library/The Royal Institution, London; 18 Mary Evans Picture Library; 19 O Rietmann/Rudolf Steiner Picture Library; 20 Bridgeman Art Library/Christie's Images, London; 21 Rex Features; 22-23 Mary Evans Picture Library; 24 Mick Rock/Cephas Picture Library; 26 Derek St Romaine; 28 Bridgeman Art Library/Roy Miles Esq; 29 Science Photo Library/ESA/PLI; 30 John Glover; 31 Harpur Garden Library; 32 Andrea Jones/Garden Exposures Photo Library; 34a Hugh Palmer/Red Cover, 34b John Glover; 35a Stephen Robson, 35b John Glover; 38 Richard Packwood/Oxford Scientific Films; 39 Mary Evans Picture Library; 40 Stephen Robson; 43 Bridgeman Art Library/British Library, London; 44 Marcus Harpur/Harpur Garden Library; 45 Andrew Lawson Photography; 46 Photos Horticultural; 47 Stephen Robson; 52 Jerry Harpur/Harpur Garden Library; 55 Science Photo Library/Space Telescope Science Institute/NASA; 57 Christy Korrow; 60 FranÁoise Sauze/Science Photo Library; 61 Adam Hart-Davis/Science Photo Library; 62 Flow Design Research Group; 65 Anthony Blake Photo Library; 66 Andrew Lawson Photography; 69 Photos Horticultural/MJK; 78a Christy Korrow,78bl Derek St Romaine, 78br Marcus Harpur/Harpur Garden Library; 80 Andrew Lawson Photography; 82 John Glover; 85-86 Photos Horticultural; 87 Derek St Romaine; 90 Andrea Jones/Garden Exposures Photo Library; 92 OPG/Stephen Robson; 93 Andrew Lawson Photography; 94bl Jerry Harpur/Harpur Garden Library, 94br Sunniva Harte/designer: Paul Thompson; 96 Tessa Traegar; 97 Marcus Harpur/Harpur Garden Library; 103 Andrew Lawson Photography; 104 Photos Horticultural; 105l John Glover, 105r Andrew Lawson Photography; 106-107 Derek St Romaine; 109l Bridgeman Art Library/Lauros-Giraudon, 109r, 110l & r Bridgeman Art Library/Lauros-Giraudon; 113 Jerry Harpur/Harpur Garden Library; 114 Photos Horticultural; 115 Dorothy Burrows/E & E Picture Library; 116 Anthony Blake Photo Library; 119 Gerrit Buntrock/Anthony Blake Photo Library; 120 John Glover/designer: Julie Toll; 123 Mary Evans Picture Library; 125 Jerry Harpur/Harpur Garden Library; 127 Steve Baxter/Anthony Blake Photo Library; 128 Andrew Lawson Photography; 131 Douglas Mason; 132 Mary Evans Picture Library; 134 Lawrence Reemer/Rudolf Steiner Picture Library; 136 Bridgeman Art Library/British Library, London; 139 Lawrence Remmer/Rudolf Steiner Picture Library.